7 STEP MINDSET MAKEOVER

Hardie Grant

BOOKS

DOMONIQUE BERTOLUCCI

7 STEP MINDSET MAKEOVER

REFOCUS YOUR THOUGHTS and
TAKE CHARGE OF YOUR LIFE

Published in 2022 by Hardie Grant Books, an imprint of Hardie Grant Publishing

Hardie Grant Books (Melbourne)
Wurundjeri Country
Building 1, 658 Church Street
Richmond, Victoria 3121

Hardie Grant Books (London)
5th & 6th Floors
52–54 Southwark Street
London SE1 1UN

hardiegrantbooks.com

 A catalogue record for this book is available from the National Library of Australia

7 Step Mindset Makeover: Refocus your thoughts and take charge of your life
ISBN 978 1 74379 802 7

10 9 8 7 6 5 4 3 2 1

Publisher: Pam Brewster
Project Editor: Brooke Munday
Editor: Kate Daniel
Design Manager: Kristin Thomas
Designer: Regine Abos
Typesetter: Patrick Cannon
Production Manager: Todd Reichner
Production Coordinator: Jessica Harvie

Colour reproduction by Splitting Image Colour Studio
Printed in China by Leo Paper Products LTD.

Hardie Grant acknowledges the Traditional Owners of the country on which we work, the Wurundjeri people of the Kulin nation and the Gadigal people of the Eora nation, and recognises their continuing connection to the land, waters and culture. We pay our respects to their Elders past and present.

For Sophia and Tobias

Many people want to achieve their goals, create new habits,
or make other positive changes in their life,
but most people find it really hard to do.

They either can't get started, get started but can't stick to it,
or end up in a cycle of making progress
and then undermining or sabotaging the progress they have made.

If this sounds like you, it is not because you're lazy,
lack commitment or whatever your preferred form of self-criticism is.
It is because you have started your quest for change in the wrong place …
you've been focusing on your actions.

If you want to change or improve your life you need to begin
by focusing on your thoughts – your mindset.

When you get your mindset right, everything else falls into place.

CONTENTS

A NOTE FROM DOMONIQUE ...

Creating lasting change in your life isn't complicated, but it can definitely feel that way when it's your life that is in the hot seat. This book is going to change that. Over the coming 7 Steps, I'll be sharing my best tips and favourite strategies for creating a mindset that makes living your best, most brilliant life something you can do with ease.

Just to be clear, I didn't say that it'll be easy. Creating these mindset shifts won't always be easy, but I promise it won't be complicated and the outcomes will be so game changing and life liberating that any effort they do require will be an effort you're happy to make.

Most people are fine with 'fine' and okay with 'okay'.
If you want to live a happy and fulfilling life,
it's important that you're not.

We are going to be taking a journey together, and like any journey there might be some bumps along the way. Sometimes the things you learn or the ideas I share might make you a little uncomfortable. They might stretch you in ways you're not used to or encourage you to step outside of your comfort zone. When this happens, please don't close this book or decide you've had enough for today. Instead, sit with your feelings and reactions and see what you can learn from them – what insights or lessons do they hold?

I'm always encouraging my clients to get comfortable with discomfort, and now it's your turn.

It will always be easier to live an ordinary life; most people are fine with 'fine' and okay with their life being just 'okay', but if you want to live a happy and fulfilling life, it's important that you don't settle for anything less than you deserve. But I don't think I need to remind you of that. I think the very fact that you've chosen to read this book tells me that living your best, most brilliant life is a commitment you've already made.

Let's dive in …

WELCOME TO THE 7 STEPS

STEP 1: DETOX YOUR DREAMS

We'll start by reclaiming the energy you've been wasting berating yourself for dreams you haven't achieved or the things you thought you would have done with your life by now but haven't. You'll know how to separate your dreams from your fantasies, so you can focus your energy on the things you really want to change or create in your life.

STEP 2: DISCOVER YOUR 'NO'

I'll show you how to create a new mindset so you can say 'no' when you need to and which eliminates the guilt and recriminations that often go with using it. Along the way you will develop a much clearer idea of what your boundaries are and have new strategies for maintaining them.

STEP 3: CHOOSE YOUR MOOD

I'm going to show you how to set yourself up to have a good day, every day, and how to make sure that you don't let anyone – or anything – take your good mood away. You'll discover how to make every day a good day regardless of what is going on in your life.

STEP 4: IGNORE THE VOICES

You'll learn how to stop worrying about what everyone else thinks or says about your life and shift your focus to making the most of it. You will completely reframe the way you think about negative feedback and criticism and what you need to do when you receive it.

STEP 5: CONFRONT THE ENEMY

I'll teach you how to stare down your fears so they never get in your way again. You'll gain a whole new insight into fear and the powerful role it plays in your life – and you'll learn exactly what you need to do when you experience it.

STEP 6: SAY GOODBYE TO YOUR 'BUT'

I'll show you how you can stop being the number one obstacle to your own success and leave your excuses behind once and for all. You'll discover what life can be like when you stop making excuses and are accountable to yourself.

STEP 7: SEE INTO THE FUTURE

In the final step, I'm going to show you how to shift your focus to what you really want from life, by understanding your values and setting clear intentions for your future. You'll know how to put your powerful new mindset to work, as we look at what you need to focus on and what you need to let go of if you want to make your best, most brilliant life your reality.

As you read and reflect on the steps, I'd love to know what your biggest insights and your favourite mindset shifts have been. I can't wait to hear your thoughts. You can find me on Instagram or Facebook via @domoniquebertolucci.

Throughout this book, I'll be sharing a whole range of tips, strategies and suggestions to help you shift your mindset. To help you put everything you're learning into action, I've created a workbook with some exercises and expanded journal prompts. I've also included some bonus resources that I just couldn't fit into this book.

The workbook is free, and you can download it as a PDF from domoniquebertolucci.com/mindset-makeover

INTRODUCING THE
ARCHITECTURE OF CHANGE

Before we get started on the 7 Steps, I want to expand on the principle I introduced right at the start – the idea that you need to prioritise creating the right mindset before you even think about taking action in your life. There is a very simple reason for this – it's your thoughts that inform your feelings, and it is your feelings that control your actions.

I call this process the *Architecture of Change* and it underpins everything I am going to share with you throughout the 7 Step Mindset Makeover.

Your thoughts inform your feelings,
and your feelings control your actions.

Although people most commonly begin any change by thinking about what actions they'll take, taking action is the last stage in a three-part process in creating lasting change in your life. Once you understand these stages, making and maintaining change will become natural and easy for you.

Just as an architect creates a 3D plan to understand how a finished project will look, you need to consider three separate aspects to get to your desired end result:

* Your Head Space
* Your Heart Space
* Your Dynamic Space

These 'spaces of change' or stages need to be considered together and not separately if you want to achieve your goals, create new habits, and make lasting change something you can do with ease.

If an architect were to design a roof without deciding on the walls that would support it or the floor that would be the foundation below it, the roof would have no support and of course it would fall down. The exact same thing happens when you attempt actions that don't have the proper support or foundation.

Let's look at those three 'spaces' in a little more detail.

YOUR HEAD SPACE: CHANGE YOUR THOUGHTS

All change begins in the mind. When you master your Head Space you will start to really think like a winner, and everything in life will become much, much easier for you.

Your thoughts control your feelings, and mastering your Head Space will mean you can identify and eliminate limits, blocks, fears or obstacles long before they have a chance to get in your way. By taking control of what you think about your goals, hopes and dreams, you will exponentially increase your likelihood of making them come true.

YOUR HEART SPACE: CHANGE YOUR FEELINGS

Your feelings govern your actions. When you master your Heart Space, feeling inspired and being motivated will become your natural and most comfortable state.

Your feelings are not good or bad – what matters is the power that you give them. Instead of expecting every feeling you have to be happy and then criticising yourself if they're not, you will be able to accept all of your feelings, without empowering them to run your life. You will also be able to create new feelings whenever you need their support.

YOUR DYNAMIC SPACE: CHANGE YOUR ACTIONS

Without action, there can be no result. When you master your Dynamic Space, you will find it much easier to do the things you need to do, to create the changes you want and get the results you desire.

Not all your actions will be things others can see. When you have mastered your Dynamic Space not only will you take action with obvious, external results, you will also make different decisions and choices. It is these countless invisible actions that will make the visible ones even easier for you to achieve.

This book is focused on the first part of the Architecture of Change, your Head Space, which is also known as – you guessed it – your mindset.

STEP 1

DETOX YOUR DREAMS

Reclaim the energy you've been wasting chastising yourself about dreams you haven't achieved or the things you thought you would have done with your life by now but haven't.

It's time to stop thinking about what you should be doing, could be doing or once might have done, and start focusing on what you really want, right here and now, in your life.

'What do you want to be when you grow up?'

This is one of the most common questions children are asked by the well-meaning older people in their lives. It's a fun question and the answers can range from the highly illuminating to the very amusing.

The good news is that we don't expect children to have any realistic sense of what they might do and who they might become when they grow up. The not-so-great news is that teenagers and adults, both young and fully grown, often aren't any more realistic in their understanding or expectations of what they might do with their life.

Personally, I bypassed the usual answers of nurse, teacher and astronaut, and went straight to the top, telling anyone who would listen that when I grew up I was going to be Wonder Woman.

I spent hours thinking about this, practising my moves with my bulletproof bracelets – made of tinfoil, of course – and daydreaming about the baddies I would capture and bring to justice with the help of my lasso of truth, also made of tinfoil.

I held on to this dream for quite possibly longer than was age-appropriate, but even when I was old enough to realise that the Wonder Woman I knew and loved was played by an actor, the glorious Lynda Carter, I still didn't really give up on the idea. I just shifted my focus from superhero to movie star, in the hope that one day I could fulfil my dream on the screen, if not in real life.

Except, of course, that it wasn't a dream.

Not really.

It was a fantasy.

✸ SEPARATE YOUR DREAMS ✸ FROM YOUR FANTASIES

The first thing you need to do if you want to detox your dreams is to separate your dreams from your fantasies.

When I tell you I wanted to become Wonder Woman and yet still haven't managed to achieve it, neither of us think anything of it. We can share a laugh and know with complete confidence that Domonique Bertolucci, born in Perth, Western Australia, was never ever going to become Diana, Princess of Themyscira. No amount of wishing, no amount of hoping and no amount of dreaming was ever going to change that – because it was nothing but a fantasy.

A child wanting to become a superhero is an obvious fantasy.

But as adults we need to let go of our fantasies too – the ideas about who we might be and what we might do that were never grounded in reality.

Fantasies are something you enjoy thinking about.
Dreams are something you are actually
willing to do something about.

Right about now, you might be thinking: 'Wait a minute, Domonique. You're a life coach. Aren't you supposed to be telling me that I can be anything I want – that the world is my oyster, that I have unlimited potential? That if I believe it, I can achieve it?'

And it's true, I absolutely, most definitely do believe that. You can do, be or have anything you really want in life. But you must be willing to work for it.

Often that means working hard, making sacrifices, going without something else you want or rising to meet challenges that are beyond the odds. It might also mean getting really clear about the essence of what it is you really want. This means getting clear about whether you are pursuing a destination or whether the journey is just as important; whether what matters is winning the prize or if being a serious contender is just as worthwhile.

But when something is a fantasy, your idea never really gets out of the gate … it hangs around as something you love thinking about but either your idea lacks substance or detail, or you lack the commitment needed to actually do something about it.

And I want you to know that's okay. It is one hundred per cent okay to have fantasies in your life – just as long as you don't treat them as something they're not. Make sure you don't mistake your fantasies for dreams and then criticise yourself or beat yourself up for failing or falling short of achieving them.

Think about all the things you've said you would do, be or have in life, but that, deep down, you now realise that you were never going to do anything about – or at least were never going to do what it really took to make them a reality in your life.

And then I want you to let them go.

✴ RELEASE YOURSELF FROM EXPECTATIONS ✴ — YOURS AND EVERYONE ELSE'S

Now that you've let go of your fantasies, we can get to work on clearing out the dreams that were never yours in the first place. I call these your 'coulda', 'woulda', 'shoulda' dreams. These are dreams and goals that you feel you are expected to achieve, but won't necessarily lead to you living a happy and fulfilling life.

Any time you find yourself saying, 'I could do this', 'I should do that', or 'If only … then I would do it' it is a clear sign that you're not talking about something you actually want to do. It really is time to stop pretending otherwise.

Society, our community, our friends and our family all have a big influence on our life. You might be conscious of some of those external influences. For generations, your family might have gone to a certain school or lived in a certain part of town. You might come from a long line of lawyers, or perhaps it was made clear that you would be the first in your family to go to university. You may have had expectations based on your gender placed on you by your family.

Let go of any dreams that were
never yours in the first place.

Our expectations can also be of our own making. You might also be consciously or unconsciously guilty of setting goals and pursuing dreams to impress other people – because you've convinced yourself it is what is expected of you or because you think that you will somehow be *less than* until you have achieved whatever it is you think you should be achieving.

✳ DON'T VIEW YOUR POTENTIAL ✳ AS AN OBLIGATION

Being gifted, talented or even having an above average skill can be a lot of pressure. Just because you can do something well doesn't mean that you have to do it.

You might have the potential to be a concert pianist, the natural skill to be an elite athlete, or the curious mind required of a scientist. But having the potential to do something is not the same as having a deep desire to do it.

I'm good at maths; I could have been an accountant. I can hold my own in an argument, and for years my dad said I should have pursued a career in law. But just because I could have or other people thought I should have, it doesn't mean that either of these paths would have been right for me. In fact, I know for certain they wouldn't have.

You don't have to pursue your potential just because you have it.

While having certain skills or talents might make other people feel excited about your potential, if these are not skills or talents you want to pursue or feel committed to developing then this is not a potential you are under any obligation to fulfil.

Trying to achieve your 'coulda', 'woulda', 'shoulda' dreams and goals often feels like pushing a boulder up a hill. You rarely make any progress and when you do, you run the risk of it crushing you.

✳ ALIGN YOUR DREAMS ✳ WITH YOUR VALUES

Knowing that you are free to pursue whatever dreams you want, the next thing you need to do is make sure the dreams you do pursue are aligned with your values. Your values are the things that matter most to you in life – the things that you judge to be important.

Everyone has their own unique set of values
and no one value is more valuable
than another.

Sometimes you might have a dream that you are working towards that doesn't feel like it is really for you, but instead is something you want to achieve for someone or something else: your family, your partner or your employer. If pursuing this is ultimately aligned with your values, then it really is still for you, even if you are not the immediate or ultimate beneficiary. Providing for your family, travelling to a loved one's wedding or giving up your Sunday sleep-in to watch your children play sport might not be what you *want* to do, but *doing* these things is how you honour your values.

Sometimes you might have an idea of something you could do or achieve, but the reality is that pursuing this would be in conflict with your values. Of course, I'm not talking about things that are against your values or feel wrong to you – I'm hoping you wouldn't even consider pursuing those. Instead,

I'm talking about those things where moving forward with one thing might take you further from something else that is important to you. When this kind of conflict is in play, you find yourself taking one step forward and two steps back, or worse, self-sabotaging your progress.

If you find that your dream is in conflict with your values, you need to examine what this dream really represents for you. Once you know the answer you will need to adjust your expectations or refine your values so they are more honestly represented.

✳ LET GO OF DREAMS ✳ THAT HAVE EXPIRED

Just like the food that lurks at the back of your fridge, some of your dreams will have a 'use by' date; the next thing I want you to do is throw out any of your dreams that have expired.

There are some things we want in life that we would happily pursue until our dying days if we thought that was what it would take to get there. But other desires are much more tightly contained within a time and place, and when that time passes it's as if those dreams have passed their 'expiry' or 'best before' date in your life. As time moves on, life moves on, and it is important that you don't let your ideas from the past prevent you from focusing on the future.

I began this chapter by talking about what you wanted to be when you grew up. As you reached the end of your teenage years and entered adulthood you were no doubt filled with ideas about all the things you might do, be or have in your life. And I really hope that at least a few of those have come to fruition for you. But just because you wanted something at eighteen doesn't mean you need to still be chasing it at twenty-five, forty-five or sixty-five, or beating yourself up because you never got there by ninety-five.

Don't let your ideas from the past
prevent you from focusing
on the future.

Growing up we are taught never to give up and that's true if you're trying to master a new skill as a child or to get the exam results you need to open a new door in your life. But there is a big difference between giving up on a dream and letting it go or setting yourself free. I speak to many people who have so much of what they need to be happy in their life but who feel like their life is inadequate in some way because they never did what they thought they would do or haven't got what they thought they would have by this point in their life.

There is no age or stage in life that comes with its own crystal ball. When you were a child your idea of what you might become and what your life might look like when you grew up was based on the information you had on hand – storybooks, children's TV and the lives of the adults in your world.

But as we get older, we still base our goals and dreams on the information we have. Some things turn out as we expected, but other things might end up completely different. Just because there is something you once wanted to do, be or have doesn't mean that you are committed to chasing after it for life.

✹ ACCEPT THAT YOUR DREAMS ✹ MAY CHANGE OVER TIME

Sometimes it's not that your dreams have expired, it's simply that they are no longer the right fit for your life. When that happens, you need to be willing to let them go.

Different things feel good at each age and stage of your life, and while sometimes it is your dreams that have expired, at other times it is you, your ideals and your values that have moved on.

Although something might have been perfect for you at one point in life, it doesn't mean it would still be the right thing for you now. But if you don't pay attention to the subtle shifts in your life you can easily put a lot of time and effort into pursuing something that ultimately won't make you happy. In fact, depending on what that is, you might even find that your achievement makes you unhappy, which would definitely be a wasted effort.

Life changes, values change, and your dreams are allowed to change too. When they do, there is no need to apologise.

I often hear my clients say things like, 'But I always said I would do that'. And yet the only person they were making their promise to was themselves. Just because you wanted something once, doesn't mean you are obliged to want it forever.

Your dreams are your own and you can
do anything you want with them –
that includes deciding to let them go.

✳ FOCUS ON LIVING A HAPPY ✳ AND FULFILLING LIFE

The last and most important thing I want you to do when it comes to detoxing your dreams is to shift your focus away from your goals and towards living a happy and fulfilling life.

It's a complete fallacy to think that a good life is one where every goal has been achieved and every dream has been fulfilled. In fact, it's a fantasy to think that it is even possible.

A perfect life is an entirely unrealistic goal,
but a happy life is within everybody's reach.

At the end of your life, it won't matter if you have achieved all your goals or made all your dreams come true. All that will matter is whether you have done enough of what is important to you to feel happy and fulfilled.

If you are fundamentally happy but there are things that you thought you would have achieved by now and haven't, you don't have to continue to pursue them. You can if you want to, but it is completely okay (and often quite sensible) to say, 'I used to want this, it didn't happen … and I'm okay with that'. You don't have to be thrilled about it; you don't even have to like it. But you are allowed to accept it.

Living a happy life is completely different from living a perfect life. A perfect life is an entirely unrealistic goal, but a happy life … well, that is something that is within everybody's reach.

KATE'S MINDSET MAKEOVER

Growing up, I always thought I was going to have lots of degrees hanging on my walls. I felt pressured by my family that it was something I should do because I could. It made me feel like I wouldn't be accomplished without it. That I needed a piece of paper to prove my worth. I still always think about the fact that I didn't finish my Master of Business Administration.

Even though I've worked in a role for ten years, had three children, changed roles twice and now find myself in a dream job, the goal of finishing my MBA has still been hanging over my head, even though I no longer need it professionally. Now that I know how to detox my dreams, I'm going to stop beating myself up about not completing my MBA.

I've realised it's time for me to let go of the fantasy that I'd go back and finish this training. I'm going to let go of making myself feel bad about the money that I spent on my Master's and then I didn't finish it. I'm at a different stage in my life and my goals have changed, so finishing my Master's … it's an outdated goal. I have all the skills I need to be successful already. I'm exactly where I need to be at this exact time.

Not all dreams are forever, and my dreams are allowed to change. And I have opportunities in my new role for training and education that will serve and support my growth and success. Letting go of this goal, this outdated dream, is a relief that has increased my confidence. Now I realise I'm okay with letting this dream go, I feel worthy, talented and competent. I value myself more than a piece of paper.

KEY INSIGHTS

STEP 1: DETOX YOUR DREAMS

1. Separate your dreams from your fantasies. A fantasy is something you enjoy thinking about; a dream is something you're willing to do something about.
2. Release yourself from expectations – yours and everyone else's.
3. Remember that just because you have potential, it doesn't mean you need to pursue it.
4. Take the time to align your dreams with your values so they take you closer to, not further from, the things that matter most in your life.
5. Throw out any dreams that have passed their 'use by' date.
6. Know that life changes, values change, and your dreams are allowed to change too!
7. Realise that it doesn't matter whether you have achieved all your goals or not; what really matters is that your life feels happy and fulfilling to you.

JOURNAL PROMPTS

★ Think of an unfulfilled fantasy you have. Be truly honest
with yourself – are you willing to do whatever you need to
do to make it your reality?

★ Have you been holding on to any dreams or goals that
aren't really compatible with your life values or the stage
of life you are at right now? What will you need to do to
release yourself?

★ Choose up to three dreams that you do want to dedicate
your energy and resources towards. Be as specific as you can
about what you want, why you want it and why now is the
right time for you.

STEP 2

DISCOVER YOUR 'NO'

Create a new mindset that not only makes it much easier to say 'no' when you want to but eliminates the guilt and recriminations that so often go with doing it.

If you feel like you're constantly being pulled in a million and one different directions and never have anything left for you, it's time for you to discover the power of 'No', 'No, thank you', 'Not now' and 'Not ever'.

One of the first words most children learn, not long after mama or dada ... is 'NO'.

By the age of two, not only do most children know exactly what 'no' means, they have already become rather proficient at using it. But somewhere along the way, between learning our first words and entering our adult lives, this skill – the ability to clearly and firmly say 'no' to the things we don't want to do – gets lost. As adults, most people find it harder and harder to say 'no' and a whole lot easier to say 'yes', regardless of how they really feel.

Does this scenario feel familiar? You find yourself running around, feeling pulled from pillar to post, trying to keep everyone else happy, to meet their needs, fulfil their requirements and comply with their requests.

At the end of the day, you realise that you've been so busy taking care of what everyone else wants and needs that you've run out of time or energy for the things that you need. You feel exhausted, frustrated and resentful.

And the worst part – whether these requests happen at home or at work – is that you know this isn't the first time it has happened and it's highly unlikely to be the last. Spending all your time and energy trying to keep everyone else happy is a sure-fire way to make sure you never have the time or energy to do the things that are going to make you happy.

The good news is that not only will learning how to create and maintain clear boundaries in your life change the way you think and feel about what everyone else wants from you, having clear boundaries will make it so much easier to actually do the things you want to do for yourself.

✳ PRIORITISE YOUR NEEDS ✳

If you want to get better at saying 'no' you first need to change the way you have been thinking about your needs in relation to everyone else's.

We are taught that it's bad to be selfish, so in our desire to be good – a good parent, a good employee, good boss, good partner, child or sibling – it's easy to fall into the habit of putting everyone else's needs first and allowing them to take precedence over your own.

But prioritising your own needs isn't selfish, it's SELF-IST.

When you are being selfish, you are putting your own needs first, to the detriment of someone else's. When you are self-ist, you are simply saying, 'My needs are important too'. Being self-ist is about recognising that while you might not always be able to put your needs at the top of your list, they definitely don't deserve to be at the bottom of it.

Deciding to be self-ist is one of the most empowering decisions you can make.

Prioritising your own needs isn't selfish
it's SELF-IST.

When you are self-ist, you recognise that your needs are valid and that they deserve to be recognised, considered, accommodated. Being self-ist is about protecting your needs with clear boundaries and maintaining those boundaries, even when you're being pressured to move them.

Recognising that you have wants and needs and that they are not always compatible with what other people want from you is illuminating. Learning how to put clear boundaries in place and to say 'no' whenever you want to or need to is liberating.

✳ LEARN TO PRESS PAUSE ✳ ON YOUR RESPONSE

Just because someone is asking something of you right now, it doesn't mean you have to say 'yes' immediately.

It's easy to feel pressured into saying 'yes' to something you don't really want to do or that doesn't fit in with your plans. It can feel like you've been put on the spot, or something about the request makes you feel guilty about refusing. If you want to release yourself from this pressure, learn to re-evaluate how you respond to a request or demand for your time, energy or attention.

Don't worry, I'm not suggesting you become rude or evasive in your response; all I am suggesting is that rather than reply instantly, you take a few minutes, hours – or depending on the request, even days – to give yourself a chance to think about the request and consciously choose the right response for you.

This approach works for all forms of requests, not just face-to-face. Next time you receive a request by email, text, iMessage, WhatsApp, Messenger or any other form of digital communication, remind yourself that just because it was an instant message, it doesn't mean it needs to have an instant answer.

Don't say 'yes' and regret it;
take the time to consider your response.

If you find yourself instinctively saying 'yes' and then immediately regretting it, you need to learn to buy yourself some time. You can do this with simple phrases like:

* ❋ I'm not sure, can I come back to you?
* ❋ Can I think about it?
* ❋ I need to check my calendar.
* ❋ When do you need to know by?

It's a good idea to build a list of phrases like these, so you can call on them any time you need them.

While you're pressing pause on your response, it's important to remember that not all of the requests for your time, energy or attention will be negative; in fact, some of them will be positively lovely. But that doesn't mean you have to say 'yes' to it right away.

Even things that you might ordinarily enjoy can feel like a chore if the timing isn't right or if they are being demanded or expected rather than suggested.

When someone says 'Jump',
stop asking 'How high?'

✳ MEET PEOPLE'S NEEDS ✳
ON YOUR TERMS

If someone is asking you to do something for them, it doesn't mean you need to drop everything and do it for them right away. While it might be ideal for them to have your attention or energy immediately, you do not have to make yourself available immediately.

And if you're worried that people might think you are being mean or not being 'nice', let me share a little story about someone who showed me how to manage this approach perfectly.

It wasn't some self-help guru, award-winning entrepreneur, or high-profile mentor of mine … it was my local dry cleaner.

If you have ever dropped off your clothing for dry cleaning you will know that it is common to be asked, 'When do you need it back by?' I don't know about you, but if they offer a next-day service, I almost always say, 'tomorrow'.

Or at least I did until I moved house, changed my dry cleaner and noticed something different and rather impressive about their approach.

I want to clarify something. When I was asked and answered that I needed the clothing the following day, it wasn't that I actually needed it then to wear – I just wanted it to be ready, so I *could* collect it. In fact, I rarely collected dry cleaning the following day and almost always when it next happened to be convenient for me.

Now, dry cleaners all around the world might be blacklisting me on account of this confession but if not the dry cleaner, I'm sure you can still find a similar example in your own life, where you accepted a speedy service because it was offered, not because you actually needed it.

The first time I visited my new dry cleaner was a Monday. As I dropped off my clothes, the guy serving me said, 'We can have this ready by Thursday, does that work for you?' I have to admit, at first I was a bit taken aback. Where was my next-day service? But the guy was super nice and smiley, and I stopped and thought about the question. 'Did Thursday work?' There wasn't anything in the pile of clothes that I had handed over that I needed back before Thursday, so I agreed, he gave me my ticket and that was that.

But as I walked away, I couldn't stop thinking about how smart his approach was.

If I'd said, 'No, that doesn't work, I need it tomorrow', or for that matter tonight, he would have met my requirements. I know this for sure because he did on several occasions. But when I said 'jump' (or in this case, 'Here's my dry cleaning') he didn't say 'How high?' He said, 'Sure, I'd love to jump – will Thursday work for you?'

In doing that, in meeting my needs at a time that worked for him, his schedule and his resources, he also freed up his company's time and resources to better serve those customers who did have an urgent request, all while not wasting their time and energy providing a quick turnaround to someone who didn't really need it.

So, what does all this mean? Other than perhaps I should read the labels when I shop and buy a few less items that say 'dry clean only'!

✹ GET CLEAR ABOUT ✹ YOUR BOUNDARIES

I think there is a hugely important lesson for everyone here.

Whenever someone says 'Jump', whatever their version of 'jump' might be on that particular occasion, you have a choice. You can say 'How high?', put your wants and needs to the side, drop whatever you are doing and meet their needs. Or, if it is something you do want to take on, you can remember my dry cleaner and say, 'Sure, I'd love to help, how about [insert whatever day and time works best for you]?'

If that doesn't work for them, they can let you know, but more often than not, when presented with this reasoned approach, people usually agree.

People will only think you are at their beck and call if you let them.

If you can see how this approach might work in your personal life but you're wondering how you might apply it at work, I've got you covered. You will find some work-based tips for what I call the 'I'll jump on Thursday' strategy in the Mindset Makeover workbook.*

---

* If you haven't got the workbook yet, you can download it free at domoniquebertolucci.com/mindset-makeover

✳ GET MUCH CLEARER ABOUT ✳ WHAT YOU WANT

One of the most common reasons people feel unable to say 'no' to all the things everyone else wants them to do is that they are not clear about their own needs or priorities – they don't know what they want.

Most people have a much clearer idea about where they would like to go on holiday than what they would like to do with their life. They don't have a clear vision or intention, they don't set goals and they go around in circles instead of moving forward.

But a lack of clarity about what you really want and what really matters to you doesn't just affect your big picture, it impacts your day-to-day life too. If you don't know what you want out of your days or your weeks, it's very easy to bend and flow with whatever anybody else wants from you instead. It is easy to become overwhelmed.

But you don't have to say 'yes', just because you don't have a reason to say 'no'. 'Because I don't want to' is a perfectly valid reason to say 'no', 'not now' or 'not ever'. You don't need to justify your decision or defend your position.

You don't have to say 'yes', just because you don't have a reason to say 'no'.

✴ OTHER PEOPLE'S REACTIONS ✴ AREN'T YOUR RESPONSIBILITY

So now that you know how to say 'no', I want to point out some of the negative reactions you may encounter when you say 'no': criticism, judgement and guilt.

It may come as a surprise to you, but other people's reactions aren't your responsibility. When someone wants your time, energy or attention it is natural for them to feel disappointed if they don't get it, and it's understandable that people might not like it if you say 'no' to their requests. But saying 'no' is your prerogative. It's your choice.

And their reactions?

Well, they are about them, not you.

Being challenged on your decision to say 'no' can feel uncomfortable, but the uncomfortable feeling that comes with being made aware of someone's disappointment in your decision is completely separate from being comfortable with the decision itself. It's important that you don't confuse the two. Make your decision calmly, deliver it clearly, and then stick to it firmly.

In life, we need to teach people how we want to be treated. If you give in or give up after a little pressure, people will learn that pressuring you is the best way to get what they want. If you are strong and clear in your 'no', they will quickly learn that you know your mind and they are wasting their time trying to change it.

If you are challenged on your decision, try saying, 'I understand my decision is disappointing to you, but I am comfortable with it'.

I deliberately use the word 'comfortable' here. It's a very respectful word – you're not saying, 'You're unhappy with me, but I don't care'; nor are you saying, 'Too bad, so sad'. Most importantly, you're not apologising. You are simply acknowledging their disappointment while holding firmly to your position.

~~~

When you say 'no' and someone is disappointed,
that is their reaction, not your responsibility.

No matter how much you care about someone, they're not going to be happy with you all of the time – but keeping them happy isn't your responsibility. When you say 'no', the person making the request of you might not like it and they may make their feelings known through their actions or their words. But it's up to you to decide if you are going to take their feelings on. You get to decide if you are going to allow their feelings to affect the way you feel about yourself.

If you find yourself in this situation, say to yourself, 'I am comfortable with my choices'. Then consciously decide not to take on anyone else's feelings as your own.

✳ DON'T LET YOUR FEELINGS ✳ RULE YOUR DECISIONS

People tell me all the time that they feel like they have to say 'yes', that they feel like they just can't say 'no', and that if they did, they would feel too guilty.

I want to show you how to shift that mindset and let go of your fear of judgement, your sense of obligation and what I call the 'disease to please', forever.

If you find yourself thinking that you need to do something, something you don't really want to do, before you answer yes – out of guilt or expectation – ask yourself why? Why do you feel you need to do it?

Of course, some of our obligations are non-negotiable: if we have a job, we need to turn up to it if we expect to get paid; if you have children you need to feed them; and you need to pay your electricity bill if you want the power to stay on.

But outside of these absolutes, most of the things we say we 'have to' do, or that we'll feel bad or guilty about if we don't, are because of an expectation: a social expectation or a self-expectation.

If you can't find a valid reason to say 'yes',
then the right answer is usually 'no'.

In Chapter 1 we looked at 'coulda', 'woulda', 'shoulda' dreams that might have stemmed from your environment, upbringing or other aspects of your social conditioning.

But goal setting and life planning aren't the only spheres in which expectations influence us. You can find yourself feeling pressured or obligated to live your day-to-day life a certain way. Over time these external expectations start to become a part of how you think things should be – regardless of how you want them to be.

Enough of that I say.

Sometimes the person you need to say 'no' to is yourself. When that happens, instead of feeling guilty, reframe your social and self-expectations with a clear statement about your own values. For example, instead of saying 'I should make lunches every day because that's what a good mother does', say 'I am a good mother because I am present with my children and spend regular quality time with them'.

Next time you find yourself feeling like you should say 'yes' to something, stop and examine why. If you can't find a valid and values-based reason to say 'yes', then the right answer is usually 'no'.

NATALIE'S MINDSET MAKEOVER

I absolutely love this step. I am someone who says 'yes' to everything when I should be saying 'no'. I'm the type of person who likes to accommodate everyone else. I don't want to cause drama or friction even if it means that I take a side step in the situation.

I say 'yes' when I know I don't have capacity to take on more clients. I say 'yes' to meeting up with a group of friends when I've already committed to two other group catch-ups that week and it puts added stress on my family responsibilities. I say 'yes' to meetings outside of my work hours.

The idea that people will think you're at their beck and call if you let them really resonates with me because in my current work situation I support people around the world, in different time zones. And recently I've noticed I'm getting more and more requests for meetings that require me to wake up at five in the morning or be up at midnight on a Zoom chat to accommodate their schedules. I've learned that I have a 'disease to please', but I now know that I don't have to! I can think of myself too! I can say 'no', and instead of dropping everything to accept meetings that aren't convenient for me, I need to set up some boundaries. I can tell a client or colleague that I will have to check my diary and propose a time that suits both of our time zones.

I've even realised I do this with friends when they contact me to arrange a coffee catch-up. In the past, I've never volunteered a time that would suit me, I've always just allowed them to suggest the time, then quietly in the background rearranged my day so it works for them. Now, if I don't have time that week, I'm going to say 'no, maybe another time' without feeling guilty. How they react isn't my responsibility.

Honestly, learning to discover my 'no' has been a real lesson for me. It's helped me reflect on my own needs as a priority. I've even made a list of things I want to do for myself each day and I'm actively making time for me to do them. I'm really pleased about that.

KEY INSIGHTS

STEP 2: DISCOVER YOUR 'NO'

1. Saying 'no' isn't selfish, it's self-ist – your needs matter too.
2. It's okay to press pause on your response while you decide whether you really want your answer to be 'yes' or 'no'.
3. When someone says 'jump', stop asking 'How high?' Instead, if you decide to meet their needs, meet them on your terms.
4. People will only think you are at their beck and call if you let them, so get clear on your boundaries.
5. You don't have to say 'yes' just because you don't have a reason to say 'no'.
6. When you say 'no' and someone is disappointed, their reaction is not your responsibility.
7. Don't let your feelings, or your fear of someone else's feelings, influence your decision. If you can't find a valid reason to say 'yes', then the right answer is usually 'no'.

JOURNAL PROMPTS

✳ Think of a situation in which you regularly say 'yes' and then regret it. Think about how this makes you feel. Think about what 'pause' phrase you are going to use to buy yourself some time to decide if 'yes' really is the right answer for you next time you are asked.

✳ Reflect on the choices you have made in the past and make a commitment to being more proactive about how you manage your boundaries moving forward.

✳ Identify one thing you're going to stop doing or decline next time you're asked.

STEP 3

CHOOSE YOUR MOOD

Set yourself up to have a good day every day, and make sure that you don't let anyone or anything take your good mood away.

While you may not be able to choose what does or doesn't happen in your day, you do get to decide how you're going to experience it. So, decide that today is going to be a good day and then do what you can to make it your reality.

Not that long ago I was walking back from my local convenience store when a ruckus on the street caught my attention. I heard this woman cursing and ranting as if her world had just fallen in. 'I can't believe it …', 'For bleep's sake …' (she didn't say bleep), 'Why does this always happen to me …' On and on she went, her anger escalating with each outburst.

Given her passion and fury, I would have been forgiven for thinking that a major catastrophe had befallen her.

Except that it hadn't.

She had received a parking ticket.

Of course, as anyone who has ever had a parking ticket will know, getting one is very annoying. It's a big waste of money for something that, with a bit more care or attention, we could have prevented. But it's not a catastrophe.

There was nothing about this woman's expensive blow-dry and European car that gave me the impression that paying her parking fine was going to mean that her children would go unfed. After snatching the ticket off her windscreen, she got into her car and accelerated away … aggressively honking her horn at someone who was crossing the street a little too slow.

I looked on in amazement at this carry-on and wondered how long it would take for her day to recover. Would she be over it in a few minutes or would she still be angry at lunchtime? Would she be ranting about it over dinner that night? Would she allow this experience to poison her entire day?

While her behaviour startled me, it didn't really surprise me. And it probably shouldn't surprise you. Although you might never have thrown a public tantrum over a parking ticket, if you're like most people, you probably have reacted to a negative experience or interaction and then allowed that reaction to overwhelm or consume you for the rest of the day.

✵ CHOOSE TO BE AN OPTIMIST ✵

One of the most important mindset decisions you will ever make is the decision to be an optimist.

When you choose to be an optimist, you are hopeful and confident about the future. You see the best possible outcome as being the most likely one. As an optimist, you assume that things are going to go well.

Being optimistic doesn't mean that you need to be blindly positive or that you can't see the risks or the downsides of any given situation. It means that while you might consider a situation from all angles, you direct your energy, attention and efforts towards the best possible outcome.

Always be confident and hopeful about your future.

When you choose to be optimistic it also means that you are choosing not to be a worrier. You do not expend energy (or waste your good mood) on worrying about things that haven't happened and, for that matter, might never happen.

As an optimist, when you feel your worries bubbling to the surface you are able to be objective about them. With a clear and calm head, you are able to evaluate if you are worried about something you can do something about, or if you have no control of the outcome at all. If you can do something about it, you can shift your energy and attention towards taking considered action, and if you can't, you can take a deep breath and accept the situation as it stands.

Being an optimist isn't just about seeing your glass as half full, not half empty. It's about looking at whatever is inside your glass and expecting it not to spill.

❋ ADOPT A POSITIVE PERSPECTIVE ❋

Like choosing optimism, this is not about being blindly positive and never seeing the flip side or downside of a given situation. It's about choosing how you want to view and experience the things that are going on in your life.

This is where the glass half full, not half empty part comes in.

Choose to see your life
in the best possible light.

The woman I told you about at the start of this chapter chose to see her parking ticket as a disaster and allowed it to ruin, if not her whole day, then certainly a decent chunk of her morning. In that moment, she had a choice. She could have seen it as a nuisance, an inconvenience or an embarrassment. Or she could have seen it as a lucky escape, knowing that her car could have been towed away for being parked where it was and what had happened instead was far less expensive and inconvenient than collecting her car from the pound.

When you adopt a positive perspective, you are making a conscious choice about how you want to see the things that are happening in your life and choosing to see them in the best possible light.

✳ HOLD ON TO YOUR GOOD MEMORIES ✳ AND ARCHIVE THE REST

When something doesn't go your way or someone lets you down, it's easy to keep dredging it up and to waste your energy churning and burning over the details. But the past is in the past and rehashing it will only bring the pain or discomfort of it into the present.

~~~

Make the decision not to hold on to
unpleasant memories.

When my children try to remind me of some cross words we've had or a time they were in strife over something, my first response is always: 'I have no idea, I don't hold on to unpleasant memories'. Eventually I remember some or all of the details, whatever the occurrence was, but they're rarely close to the surface and it almost always requires some digging through my memory before the event can be recalled with any clarity.

For me, this is not just the case for the little things that go on in my day-to-day life. Larger, more significant upsets are filed deep in my memory archives only to be accessed if or when I want to bring them up too.

Before you start worrying about my memory, let me assure you that this isn't an accident – and it's not age related. It's not that I forget negative experiences the minute they've happened. I don't. But I do take anything I can from the experience – wisdom, insights, lessons learned the hard way – then make a conscious decision to just let it go. I don't bring it up over and over. I don't hash through the details, as if by remembering them precisely I could change the specifics of them. And I definitely don't agonise over what might have been.

It is what it is.

I remind myself of that and then I let it fade from view.

✳ DECIDE TODAY IS GOING ✳
TO BE A GOOD DAY

Once you've changed the way you think about the past, you can shift your focus to the present.

One of the first things you need to do if you want to have a good day, every day, is to decide to have a good day. If that sounds incredibly simple, it's because it really doesn't need to be any more complicated than that.

*Focus your attention on your intention
and do what you can to make it your reality.*

When you wake up each morning, remind yourself that today is a 'good-to-be-alive-day' – simply because you are alive.

Then, before you get out of bed, set a clear intention for your day. Consciously decide how you want to experience your day: how you would like it to unfold, how you'd like to feel and what you'd like to be able to say about it when you get back into bed that night.

Once you know how you would like to feel, you can then make choices throughout the day that give you the best chance of making those feelings real.

When hiccups and challenges present themselves, as they invariably will, remind yourself of the intention you set and reconnect with that decision. You can then consciously choose your reactions and responses, knowing how you want to feel about your day and the positive feelings you will utilise.

At the end of each day look back over it and recap, review and reflect. Think about how your day unfolded, what went well and what didn't go so well, and what you would like to do differently tomorrow. This isn't a last-minute chance to criticise yourself or beat yourself up before the lights go off, it's an important part of being able to be more mindful about how you are living your life and the choices you are making throughout your day.

As you complete your recap of your day, if you want to really give your mood one last boost, ask yourself these two questions: What gave me joy today? What am I grateful for today?

Expressing your gratitude and consciously identifying sources of joy not only feels good and gives your mood a boost in the moment, it also trains your mind to make maintaining an optimistic mindset and choosing a positive perspective something that comes much more naturally to you.

✳ TAKE OWNERSHIP OF ✳ YOUR EXPERIENCE

Nobody has the power to ruin your mood or, for that matter, your entire day, unless you let them.

Nobody can make you feel bad without your permission, so whenever something goes wrong, or someone says something that hurts your feelings or does something that makes you feel angry, pause for a moment before you react. Ask yourself, 'How do I want this situation to impact me?' and then consciously choose your reaction based on your answer.

While you can't control what will or won't happen during your day, you do get to decide how you want to experience it. You can let people bump you off course, leaving you feeling like a victim of the circumstance of your day and the people in it, or you can stay focused on the intentions you set when you started your day and choose only to only engage in thoughts and feelings that support them.

There are so many different things that can go wrong or get your back up on any given day, but they really don't have to.

Don't let the outside 'noise' in your life take over.
Choose your mood and don't let anyone
or anything take it away from you.

If someone upsets you or says the wrong thing to you, decide how you want to experience it. Remember that unkind or hurtful words are rarely about you and almost always about how the person saying them is feeling about themselves.

If someone makes a mistake or lets you down, instead of raging against the injustice of it all, remind yourself that most people are doing their best most of the time – they probably weren't trying to ruin your day, it's just that their best wasn't quite up to scratch this time.

Instead of doubling down on the negativity you've experienced, try to find forgiveness and compassion – they're obviously feeling pretty miserable if they need to take it out on you. And if you're not quite up to forgiveness and compassion in that moment, then disengage from their comments and consciously choose not to actively engage in the hurt or frustration you're experiencing.

This is not about bottling up your feelings or stuffing them down. Remember the Architecture of Change – it's your thoughts that control your feelings, not the other way around. This is about consciously generating new feelings, by choosing how you want to think about the situation you're experiencing.

It's not always possible to stop feelings of hurt or anger in a situation. But even though your feelings might be unpleasant or uncomfortable, you still get to decide how much influence you would like them to have over you.

✹ COMMIT TO YOUR HAPPINESS ✹

It is no-one else's job to make you happy and even if they try they'll never succeed if you're not already feeling happy within yourself. Your happiness is your responsibility.

As I wrote in *The Happiness Code*, happiness begins with a choice. The minute you make the decision to be happy, you will have taken your first step towards becoming happier. Your perspective shifts and you start to see your world from the vantage point of someone who is happy.

Happiness is a choice.
Choose to be happy
and you will be.

Of course, choosing to be happy isn't the only thing that you need to do, but unless you make the conscious decision to be happy, all your other efforts could be wasted. Being happy isn't something that you become 'one day', or something that you get when you cross off enough things on your life's to-do list. You don't decide, 'Being happy, hmm … I think I'll give that a try next Tuesday'. True happiness is a way of life. It's a commitment.

A big part of that commitment is making sure you don't undermine or compromise it. This means making conscious choices to support your happiness, not just about the things you do, but the thoughts you have and the feelings they generate.

✳ DECIDE HOW YOU WANT TO ✳ FEEL ABOUT YOUR LIFE

One of the most common misunderstandings people have about life is that it is something that happens to you.

You're born, various experiences happen to you, and then, hopefully at a ripe old age, you die.

But that's not quite how it works.

I believe living a happy and fulfilling life is as much about what you create, or *make happen*, as what you do with the various things that *just happen* – life is what you make of it.

We all know a story about someone who 'had everything' but was never really happy, who squandered their good fortune or let their advantages go to waste. And we are uplifted by stories of people who have overcome every disadvantage to rise up and shine and have achieved extraordinary things in their lives.

*You can't choose what happens in your life,
but you can decide how you want to feel about it.*

For most of us, the truth of our experience will be somewhere in between. Every well-lived life has ups and downs, highs and lows, victories and heartbreak. Good days and bad. I've had mine and I'm sure you have had yours. Making conscious choices about how you experience things means that you are the one who is in charge of how you feel about your life.

ASHLEY'S MINDSET MAKEOVER

I often let my frustration in situations get the better of me and ruin my day. I realise this now. And I've also realised how this can have a really significant impact on my life. I really liked this step because I needed it.

Learning that I needed to choose to be happy was like a light-bulb moment for me. I'm always wishing I was happy or happier. I just wanted to feel happier more often, you know ... so Step 3 helped me realise I need to actually *choose* happiness. I need to find those actions that enable me to take a step back. If I start to get negative or start allowing others to control my feelings, I need to take a deep breath, not let frustration get the better of me, and reclaim my happiness.

It's amazing how just by setting the intention with myself I can accept the situation for what it is and choose to let go. I can continue with my plan to be and remain positive, energetic and calm.

Crappy things will happen from time to time but life will still be okay – I can choose to be happy as my natural default to help me face whatever life throws my way.

Actually, it's funny you shared the parking ticket story because today was a day when I really needed to choose my mood. I was running for a train last night on my way home from work, wearing some very high heels, and I took a huge tumble. Not only did I miss the train, but I sprained my ankle. When it happened I could feel my mood shifting and today I can't walk or do the things I needed to do – and I had a busy day planned.

I could have chosen to be stroppy and cross because there's so many things I want to do, and I was totally embarrassed by falling over in public. But I've chosen to be happy and lie on my couch and have people fetch me things. I've really truly chosen to hold on to the good and let go of the bad – and I'm happy!

KEY
INSIGHTS

STEP 3: CHOOSE YOUR MOOD

1. Choose to be optimistic – always be hopeful and confident about your future.

2. Adopt a positive perspective and see your life in the best possible light.

3. Train your memory to hold on to the good parts and archive the rest.

4. Decide today is going to be a good day and do what you can to make that intention your reality.

5. Consciously choose thoughts that generate the feelings you want and need to have.

6. Know that your happiness is your responsibility – commit to it and take that commitment seriously.

7. Remember, you can't choose what happens in your life, but you do get to decide how you want to feel about it.

JOURNAL PROMPTS

* Regardless of what is going on in your life, are you aware of all you have to be grateful for? Make a note of at least three things you are grateful for in your life and keep that list close to your heart and mind; add to it whenever you can, ideally every day.

* Think of a time when someone did or said something that upset you. Reflect on the choices you made about how much impact or influence you allowed that experience to have on your day – and your life.

* Choose one thing you are going to remind yourself of next time you feel like you need to give your mood a boost.

STEP 4

IGNORE THE VOICES

Stop worrying about what everyone else says or thinks about you and your life – focus your energy on making sure that you make the most of it.

Silencing your inner critic is important, but it's equally important that you find a way to block both your heart and your ears to your external critics too. Unless you make the decision not to listen to these voices, regardless of whether they are well-meaning or malicious, they will quickly drown out any positive thoughts you might have.

I often think of a conversation I had a long time ago with a mentor of mine. We were talking about the fear of judgement, of not being liked. I can't remember the specifics of my concern, whether I was worried about someone in particular or if it was just a general fear of putting my head above the parapet, but I remember my mentor's response with total clarity.

He said, 'Some will, some won't, so what'.

Some will.

Some won't.

So what.

His message was clear. While some people would think positively about me, others might not. But the real question I needed to answer was, 'Why did it matter?'

Why did I care? Why was I letting, not even a negative opinion, but a potential negative opinion get in my way? Why was I wasting my time and my energy thinking about it? These were powerful questions then and they're powerful questions now. Why should someone else's opinion or judgement of you matter so much? Why should it matter more than your opinion or judgement of yourself? Why would you prioritise their thoughts, feelings or opinions over your own?

✳ WHEN SOMEONE JUDGES YOU, ✳ IT'S ABOUT THEM NOT YOU

When it comes to reframing your feelings about being judged or receiving criticism or negative feedback, the first thing you need to do is to accept – and believe – that someone else's judgement of you is about them, not you; it's about their thoughts and feelings, their values and ideals.

Regardless of whether you are receiving uninvited criticism or feedback on an idea you've aired, or you feel like you are being put down for a decision you've made, the first and foremost thing you need to remember is that it's not about you.

It is not about you.

When I'm training people to coach others to be the best they can be, one of the sayings we use over and over again is: 'No thoughts, no feelings, no values, no judgements'. As a coach you don't want to push your agenda onto your clients; you don't want to be viewing their situation through the filter of your experience and you can't assume your client is honouring the same set of values as you are.

But until everyone else learns how and when to give feedback so that it is appropriate and well received, the onus is on you to make sure that others' thoughts, feelings, values and judgements don't have a negative impact on you. Although it might be presented as being about you, and the person who is providing you with this input might truly believe in their heart that it is about you, it never is. It's about them.

People will criticise you, judge you or put you down because they are feeling insecure or because you've challenged one of their limiting beliefs. They may be negative about your choices because they wouldn't be comfortable with them or because your choices are in conflict with their values. Your decisions might challenge their fears or disrupt their status quo or take them way outside of their own comfort zone.

There are so many different reasons why someone might decide to be critical, but understanding why it has occurred is far less important than recognising who it's really about when it does. Once you realise that it is not really about you, nothing anybody says about you or your ideas will ever have quite the same power to hurt you again.

✳ OPINIONS ARE NOT FACTS ✳

Whether someone is criticising you or trying to be helpful – and the two often get confused by the person giving the feedback – their opinion is just their opinion. It is not a fact.

Of course, there are exceptions to this, but unless the feedback you are being given is on a maths equation or some other scenario that has an absolute right and wrong – or by your boss, a competition judge or someone else whose opinion is vital to the success of your endeavour – all you are being presented with is their perspective. Opinions often get presented as absolutes ('My way is the right way'), presented as facts or as what you should do. But regardless of how someone's opinion is presented, it is still just an opinion. Nothing less. And most certainly nothing more.

Opinions are often presented as facts,
but that doesn't mean that they are.

✳ LET NEGATIVE OPINIONS ✳
SLIDE RIGHT OFF

Just because someone is offering you their opinion, it doesn't mean you have to accept it.

When we were children, it was the role of the adults in our lives – parents, carers, teachers and so on – to teach us right from wrong. It was their job to help shape our values, inform our opinion and frame our world view. But now that you are an adult, that job comes down to you. It is no longer the role of the other adults in your life to shape you – no matter how much they would like it to be.

You get to decide what is right or wrong for you. You get to decide on all the big things in your life: what you believe, who you love, where you work, what you do with your money, how you raise your children or who your friends are. And you get to decide on the little things too: what you wear, what you eat and where you like to holiday – the list goes on and on.

Other people in your life may have opinions on all of your choices, but unless you have asked for their opinion, you are under no obligation to consider it. Even if you have asked for their opinion, you only need to listen – you are under no obligation to accept it. And when someone expresses a negative view about you, you can ignore it. I'm serious!

Unless you have asked someone for their opinion,
you don't even need to consider it –
unless you want to.

I want you to imagine your self-esteem as a non-stick pan, like a frying pan coated in Teflon, where criticisms, judgements and negative opinions just slide right off. Can you feel how much lighter life would be if you were able to take this approach and make the decisions that you knew were right for you, without taking on all the unhelpful and unkind input about your choices? You don't need to debate it, you don't need to justify your own choice or position, you don't need to be deflated by it, hurt or let down by it. Most importantly, you don't need to avoid it. All you need to do is take a deep breath and ignore it.

✳ DON'T BE AFRAID OF WHAT OTHER ✳ PEOPLE THINK OF YOU

So many people hold themselves back or limit their potential because they are afraid of what others will think; they're afraid of being criticised, judged or talked about in a negative way. Some people do it consciously, not taking action or making a change because of what so-and-so might say. Others do it subconsciously, holding themselves back without even realising they're doing it. What a waste of life's opportunities.

*Don't let other people's opinions of you
influence your opinion of you.*

Once, during a radio interview, the topic of wanting to be liked came up and when I said, 'I really don't care what other people think about me', the interviewer challenged me.

'Surely you want to be liked', she said. 'Everybody wants to be liked.' And so I clarified: 'I absolutely prefer to be liked. In an ideal world, everybody I encounter would have nothing but positive thoughts about me. But I don't *care* about their opinions. Whether they like me or not doesn't change the way I feel about me'.

✳ CHOOSE YOUR CHEERLEADERS ✳

Okay, I know I just said that I don't care what other people think about me, but there are a few exceptions to this. There is a small group of people whose views do matter to me. A very small group. I trust them to understand the values that I hold dear and to hold me fully accountable to them. And I trust them to support me unconditionally.

Those in my inner circle offer me wise, unbiased, non-judgemental support when I need it, and if someone in this group tells me I'm out of line, or making poor decisions, I take it very seriously. But these people are the exception.

Create an inner circle of people
whose opinions you trust completely.

When choosing your inner circle, the people whose opinions you do welcome, it's important that you choose them mindfully. It doesn't need to be your mother, your father, your sister or a friend you've known your whole life. It certainly doesn't need to be your mother-in-law or someone you know from work.

Choose your cheerleaders and choose them wisely. But even when you know whose counsel you do trust, whose opinions you do value, you are still not under any obligation to accept those offered opinions if you don't feel that they are right for you.

✳ BECOME YOUR OWN BIGGEST FAN ✳

While we are talking about whose opinion does or doesn't matter, there is one person whose opinion of you matters most of all – *you*.

It's easy to feel good about yourself when someone is telling you how good you are. But if your self-belief and sense of self-worth are dependent on other people's favourable opinion of you, you can't expect to feel good when those words are not forthcoming. Sourcing your self-esteem externally is not sustainable. You can't rely on compliments or positive feedback to make you feel good about yourself, and you will be wasting a lot of your life if you let negative feedback or criticism bring you down.

It's not enough just to ignore the external voices, all the criticism and judgement, and all the unsupportive, 'helpful' feedback that you never wanted or asked for in the first place. While ignoring all those voices is an important way to protect your self-esteem, it won't help nearly enough if you are constantly doing the same hatchet job on yourself.

Your self-esteem is one of your most valuable resources so make sure you nurture, encourage, support and protect it.

One of the most important things you can do to boost your self-belief is to start listening to your internal conversations and self-talk. How do you speak to yourself? Are you your own biggest fan or your harshest critic? Are you your own cheerleader, cheering yourself on regardless of whether it looks like you are on the winning team, or are you the first to berate yourself when things don't go according to plan?

One of the greatest gifts you can give yourself is self-belief, with as much emphasis on the word 'self' as there is on the word 'belief'. Not everything in life can be counted on to go your way. It may be that you miss out on getting the job you wanted, get dumped when you thought you were loved, lose what you thought was a winning pitch, miss out on an invite or get turned down by the bank for a business loan. Regardless of what is going on in your life, it is important not to let setbacks impact your self-belief.

If your belief in yourself is dependent on the approval or reinforcement of others, then every time something doesn't go your way, your self-esteem will be left battered and bruised. When you believe in yourself unconditionally, your self-esteem is independent of the opinions of others, and it won't matter what anyone else says or thinks.

Even though you didn't get the job or didn't win a pitch, it doesn't mean that you or your ideas don't have great potential. If a relationship ends unexpectedly, it doesn't mean that you aren't a great catch; if someone doesn't think to include you in their life, it's their loss, not yours.

While most people would admit to engaging in self-criticism or negative self-talk some of the time, it is only when they really start paying attention to their internal dialogue that they realise they are engaging in negative self-talk almost all the time.

It's very difficult to feel good about yourself if you are constantly thinking negative thoughts. If you want to maintain a healthy level of confidence and self-belief, you need to put a stop to these messages and take back the ownership of the chat inside your head.

✸ NEVER SPEAK TO YOURSELF ✸ MORE HARSHLY THAN YOU WOULD TO A SMALL CHILD

There's a story I've told in several of my books and on hundreds of stages about a time when I was walking in the park, and I heard a woman berate her son for climbing a tree and then being too scared to climb back down.

'Stop being so pathetic', 'You really are being stupid', 'What a wimp you are.' On and on she went as this little boy cried in fear and humiliation. I felt sick listening to her words and was very relieved when her companion eventually came over and helped the boy down from the tree.*

When I tell this story to a live audience, there is always a sharp intake of breath as I share those cruel words. The audience is shocked. We all know that is no way to speak to a child or, for that matter, to anyone you would like to get the best out of.

As an adult, if you are caring for a child, in that moment, you are the guardian of their self-esteem. That's why those harsh words from that woman feel so shocking. We all know hearing those words would have been crushing for that little boy.

---

* If you want to listen to the whole story about the boy in the tree, check out the workbook that goes with this book.

Why on earth would you ever say them to yourself?

Yet how often do you speak to yourself like that? How often do you call yourself an idiot, say that you're being stupid, criticise and berate yourself, or put yourself down? Instead of allowing this to be your default form of self-talk, protect your self-esteem, and only ever speak to yourself with kindness, patience and respect.

You are the guardian of your self-esteem.
Guard it wisely.

MATTHEW'S MINDSET MAKEOVER

Learning to ignore the voices is a daily battle in my head. I like to think that I don't care what other people's opinions are, but my automatic response is caring how I'm viewed by others and whether I'm accepted.

When I was a kid I was picked on at school for my height and my glasses, so I've had to work a lot on my confidence.

This step made me realise just how much I still hold on to these things and how I need to shift my mindset going forward to really feel good about myself and make change in my life. Even if I'd prefer that people like me, I don't necessarily need it. There's a difference. And even if people are being critical of me, or have been critical of me, I don't need to take it on board. That's their opinion coming out – they're projecting their own fears and beliefs and ideals onto me. Often, it's about them anyway.

Ignoring the voices has been eye-opening for me: trying to be liked takes a lot of time and energy – sometimes it even feels like work. I shouldn't be placing so much importance on it; I shouldn't be worried if people don't like me, as long as I like and support myself.

I need to learn how to cheer myself on and only seek advice from people I truly trust. And even then, only I am responsible for me and how I feel about myself and how I treat myself. They can offer advice, but I can choose whether I accept it or not.

Self-doubt is one of the loudest voices I have to ignore. Moving forward, I will try my best to be my own compass and just go with what I feel deep down is the right thing to do. I've always wanted to start my own YouTube channel, but haven't because I'm worried about what people think, even those in my life that support me and want me to do it – it makes me feel self-conscious. But maybe it's time I listened to my cheerleaders, ignored the voice of self-doubt and just did it. No more holding back.

KEY
INSIGHTS

STEP 4: IGNORE THE VOICES

1. Know that when someone judges or criticises you, it's about them not you.
2. Remember that other people's opinions are just their opinions, they're not facts.
3. Develop emotional Teflon and let criticism and negative opinions slide right off.
4. Stop worrying about what other people might think of you, and don't let the fear of being judged hold you back.
5. Choose a group of personal cheerleaders whose opinions of you matter; choose them wisely and trust them completely.
6. Become your own biggest fan – the only person's opinion about you that really matters is yours.
7. Never speak to yourself more harshly than you would to a small child – you are the guardian of your self-esteem so guard it wisely.

JOURNAL PROMPTS

✳ Think of a time when other people told you that you were wrong, but deep down you knew you were right. Reflect on how you learned from this experience.

✳ Think about your personal group of cheerleaders. Who are they and why does their opinion hold value to you?

✳ Think of three things you can tell yourself that will help you to boost your self-confidence, nurture your self-esteem and help you feel good about who you are.

CONFRONT THE ENEMY

Understand the role fear plays in your life and know exactly what to do when you experience it.

The biggest thing holding most people back is fear – fear of success, fear of failure and fear of everything in between. But experiencing fear doesn't have to stop you. It's time to face your fears and liberate yourself from the power they have held over you.

Fear is a natural and normal part of life, but many people misunderstand it and spend their lives trying to avoid it.

I don't mean fears and phobias like spiders, flying, bridges, heights or things that go bump in the night! The kind of fears I am talking about here are much deeper – fears in your soul, which will eat away at your confidence and self-belief if you let them. But as unpleasant as they are, you really don't need to hide from these fears. They are not a sign that something bad is about to happen; in fact, they're often quite the opposite.

✳ FEAR SIMPLY MEANS THAT ✳ SOMETHING IS IMPORTANT

The first thing you need to know as you shift the mindset about fear and the power it holds in your life is that fear is simply your subconscious letting you know something is important.

I've always been someone other people describe as fearless. I travelled on my own from a young age, took on big jobs that I was underqualified for and stood up to bullies when I had to. But I'm not fearless – rather, over the years I've become highly skilled at confronting and disempowering my fears so they never have the chance to stop me.

I knew that I shouldn't let my fears stop me from doing what I wanted, but I never fully understood the true nature of them – that they were a sign that something was important to me – until I was presented with the opportunity to explore a life-long dream. The fear that I experienced in that moment was so strong, so visceral, that I thought I might vomit from it. Thankfully I didn't, but after I had reflected on and fully processed this experience, when and why we experience fear made sense to me in a much deeper way than it ever had before.

In the first chapter of this book, I shared the story of how as a teenager I had wanted to be an actor ... or to be more precise, a movie star. After an early start as a rather unsuccessful fashion model – I was never thin enough, and I was told my smile was much too wide! – there was nothing in my career path that gave the slightest clue that I was still harbouring this dream to be on screen.

But I was.

Deep down it was my big 'What if?' What if I had chosen the wrong path, what if I was wasting my life or missing my calling?

It nagged away at me.

Sometimes it was loud and other times more of a whisper, but it never really went away.

When I was twenty-nine, after a particularly demanding project for an investment bank in London, I knew I needed an extended holiday: a mini-sabbatical. Although I was initially tempted to follow the path many of my colleagues were taking – going trekking in the Himalayas, spending weeks in yoga retreats and other similar adventures – a little voice inside told me this was my moment.

I decided to spend my summer in a full-time film and television program at NYU – New York University (and by living in the Big Apple I would have the chance to fulfil two dreams at once). The course I had chosen required an interview. Not an audition per se, but a face-to-face meeting with the director of the program. This was a long time before Zoom, but I was able to make an appointment to meet him on my next work trip to New York.

The day of the meeting came. I woke excited, got dressed in my carefully planned, chic, all black, I-could-be-the-next-big-thing outfit and set off on foot. The meeting was only a few blocks away and I started off with a spring in my step. As I got closer to the address, I'll admit that my step wasn't quite so springy. But it was nothing serious – nothing that couldn't be put down to ordinary everyday nervousness.

But that all changed as the building came into sight.

The feeling came on suddenly and it was overwhelming. My feet were rooted to the spot, and I felt like I was going to throw up on my newly purchased, I-could-be-the-next-big-thing shoes.

At first I didn't even recognise the feeling.

It was so much bigger than nerves. I was terrified.

But at the same time, the terror was non-specific. I wasn't afraid I'd forget my lines; I hadn't had to learn any. And I wasn't worried they wouldn't like me or that I'd fail to impress them with my enthusiasm; I'd interviewed and won jobs in some of the toughest financial institutions in London – I wasn't feeling intimidated.

So what was this feeling?

I took a deep breath and another (and thanked my lucky stars that I had time up my sleeve to compose myself). I listened to my body. I listened to my heart, and I listened to my soul.

And what I heard as clear as day was, 'This is it!'

'This could really be IT!'

And suddenly it all made sense.

This was my chance to follow my dreams. Being accepted into this course could change everything. If I succeeded my dreams would be, if not in reach, then definitely in sight … But if I failed – if it turned out I didn't have the talent I needed – I would need to let my dream go … and then how would I fill that void?

It would all begin with this meeting. The significance of the situation hit me.

This mattered. It mattered in a way that nothing in my career had ever mattered before. And that was what this overwhelming feeling was trying to tell me.

I took a few more breaths, and in I went.

Your fears are your subconscious letting you know that something is important.

No matter how hard we try, we can never predict the future, and it turned out my participation in this program mattered in an entirely different way than I had thought it would.

Although I loved the program, I didn't feel like acting was my calling. And although I enjoyed working through my scenes, I wasn't sure I'd want to play them night after night or spend whole days filming them in three-minute increments. I finally realised that being an actor wasn't something I needed to do with my life and that being a movie star had never been my dream, it was just a fantasy.

I enjoyed three of the best, most challenging and exciting months of my life in New York City doing that course, but in the end I kissed my fantasy goodbye and never looked back.

If I hadn't taken a deep breath and gone into the meeting I never would have found this out. If I'd falsely interpreted my fear as an instinct or intuition that the program wasn't right for me, I never would have known. And if I'd never been willing to step out of my comfort zone and enrol in the course in the first place that dream-cum-fantasy of mine might still be playing on an endless loop in my mind.

✳ DON'T GIVE YOUR FEARS MORE ✳
POWER THAN THEY DESERVE

Experiencing fear is your mind telling your body that something is important to you – listen carefully for that message.

But not all fears are the same.

When I say don't let your fears stop you, I mean the type of uncomfortable feeling you get when facing something different or new – butterflies in the stomach, tightness in your chest, feeling nervous about doing well or anxious about the outcome. I'm not talking about ignoring an intuition or instinct you might have that something is not right, even dangerous. When you feel that kind of fear, you need to pay very close attention and then act on it.

People often ask me how you can tell the difference between an emotive fear, the kind that is driven by stepping outside of your comfort zone, and an instinctive or intuitive fear, the kind that is warning you something is really wrong. My answer is to look for the feeling in your body. More often than not, you will experience your emotive fears, the kind that ultimately are a good sign, in your stomach and occasionally rising up to your chest. These healthy fears have a very specific anchor point in your body. They begin in your stomach, hence the expressions 'feeling sick to your stomach' and 'in the pit of my stomach' and expand through your body from there.

An intuitive or instinctive fear will be felt at a cellular level; it's as if every cell in your body is trying to warn you that something is not right. I describe these intuitive feelings as something I could feel 'right down to my fingertips'. When you experience fear in this way, you should pay close attention to it and act on it accordingly. Instinctive or intuitive fear is serious. It is your subconscious warning you of imminent danger, and whether that danger is physical, mental or emotional you want to get away from it as fast as you can.

What you don't want to do, however, is give every fear you have this level of power.

Your head can turn anything into a drama, but your body will know when it is real. Don't just listen to your gut, listen to every cell in your body. Just because the thought of doing something makes you feel nervous, uncomfortable or outright terrified, it doesn't mean you shouldn't do it.

Regardless of what your emotive fears are,
they really don't have to get in your way.

The fact is, most of the fears you experience will be emotive and driven by your feelings. Instead of giving in to these fears, simply acknowledge them, understand the insight they hold and move on.

✻ DON'T GO INTO BATTLE ✻ WITH YOUR FEARS

The healthiest approach you can have to acknowledging your fears is one of benign curiosity. Don't deny your fears or try to suppress them. Don't judge your fears and say, 'Isn't it silly that I feel …' or 'I know it's stupid, but …' And whatever you do, don't make it your mission to conquer them, or make conquering them a prerequisite for taking action. Instead, be curious about them.

Your fears don't need to be defeated.
You just need to own them and let them
accompany you along your way.

When you find yourself experiencing fear, say to yourself, 'Isn't this interesting … I wonder what my subconscious is trying to tell me …' or 'What lesson does this fear have for me?' Don't try to force the answer. Just listen to your mind, your heart and your soul and trust that the answer will come.

When I discover a fear, I say to myself: 'I am experiencing fear, how interesting …' 'I'm feeling intimidated by this meeting … Isn't that interesting.' It is not good. It is not bad. It is simply cause for curiosity. This neutral language will disempower your fears. They are not good or bad, and you are not a better or worse person for having them. They are simply an interesting development and an invitation to an important discovery.

✳ DON'T LET YOUR FEARS ✳ STAND IN YOUR WAY

Even if you are experiencing fear, it doesn't mean you have to stop what you are doing or choose a different path. You don't need to expend a lot of time or energy understanding or getting to grips with your fears; when it comes to taking action all you need to do is acknowledge your fears and carry on regardless. Experiencing fear is a natural, normal part of life. Allowing your fears to get in your way is a choice and one you don't have to make!

People waste so much energy denying their fears or, worse, fighting with them. The key is to own up to them so that you can address them. Just because the thought of doing something makes you feel nervous, uncomfortable or outright terrified, it doesn't mean you shouldn't do it. Instead of letting your feelings get in your way, take a deep breath and be brave.

Sometimes an acknowledgement is all you need to disempower your fear entirely. If you deny the fear or try to overcome it without first accepting that you feel it, you waste an inordinate amount of energy trying to conquer it – which might not be necessary. Either way, the best course of action is always to acknowledge your fear and keep moving through it.

Sometimes acknowledging your fears is all you need to disempower them.

Your fears, like all of your other feelings, are yours. You are one hundred per cent entitled to them and you should never feel as though you have to apologise for them.

Instead, acknowledge your fear, and accept that while it might not be particularly pleasant to experience it is how you are feeling … then carry on regardless.

✴ UNDERSTAND THE REAL SOURCE ✴ OF YOUR FEARS

One of my all-time favourite quotes is from the movie *Strictly Ballroom*. I love so many things about that film, but most of all I love the line, 'A life lived in fear is a life half lived'.

Fear of failure has many guises, but it is most powerful in holding you back from achieving your potential. At first, you might not even recognise that it is fear holding you back. You might think your concerns and worries are legitimate, but if deep in your heart you feel you are not achieving your potential a fear of failure is probably getting in your way.

While most people are familiar with the concept of 'fear of failure', a lesser known but equally disempowering fear is the fear of success. You might be thinking, 'How could I be afraid of success?' 'Why would I be afraid of achieving what I want?' The changes your success will bring can be quite daunting, and subconsciously you might be questioning whether or not you will be able to manage the impact of your success. You might be concerned about becoming busier, receiving more attention and having increased responsibility, or you might simply be worried that you won't like the future you are creating when you get there!

While fear of failure often results in a lack of action, one of the most common manifestations of the fear of success is self-sabotaging behaviour – when you become your own worst enemy and start doing things that actively move you away from your goal.

Understanding the fears you have about success is just as important as learning to move through your fear of failure.

✹ DON'T BE AFRAID OF DISRUPTING ✹ YOUR STATUS QUO

If nothing changes, nothing changes – and yet the biggest fear for many people is the fear of disrupting their status quo.

Life is a delicate balance. The more you have to juggle the harder it is to keep all those balls in the air. Subconsciously you may be worried that pursuing your goals, your hopes and your dreams will compromise or sabotage the things you hold dear – the things that are working in your life, the things that are important in your life.

But it doesn't have to be that way.

Honour your values and stop worrying about everything else.

Take the time to understand what you value and what you need to do to protect the things that matter to you. Make this your priority and then stop being afraid of it impacting anything else.

✳ BECOME FRIENDS WITH ✳ YOUR FEARS, OR AT LEAST GET BETTER ACQUAINTED

You've heard the saying, keep your friends close and your enemies closer … Well, I feel that way about fears. Your fears will only have power over your life if you try to run from them, deny them or surrender to them. The only way to keep them in their rightful place is to take the time to properly get to know them. You don't need to judge them or go into battle with them. Instead, look for the lesson within them.

To shift your feelings you need to create new thoughts, and the best way to do this is to reframe them by grounding them in logic and to reform them with affirmations – positive, personal, present-tense statements about what you would like to feel.

If you want to change the way you feel about your fears,
first you need to change the way you think about them.

Affirmations are an easy to use, yet seriously powerful mindset tool and I've included a guide to creating yours in the workbook that goes with this book.

In my case, before my interview in New York, I could have used affirmations like:

I am confident and my interview is a success.

I am excited about opening the door to this new opportunity.

I have been offered a place on the program of my dreams.

Once you understand that your fears are an insight into what is important to you, you can consciously craft new thoughts – a new mindset – to help you to move forward in spite of them.

KATHY'S MINDSET MAKEOVER

This step offered a huge insight for me. I really need to sit with my fears. I need to get to know them rather than letting them blindly influence me without question. I know that's something I've been guilty of.

I feel like I've achieved most of what I wanted to do in my life, but a few years ago I had a couple of big failures. Or at least what I see as failures.

I set out on long-distance hikes, but never actually finished them. One of them was about 1200 kilometres — and I did about 400. The other one was 800 kilometres and I did about half.

I never actually accomplished what I'd set out to do, and while I had to pull out for unavoidable reasons, when I think about starting on that journey again, of going on future long-distance hikes, I'm very reluctant to commit. I'm almost consumed by fear that I'll fail again. It's sat uncomfortably with me ever since. I feel pretty yucky when I think about it. Maybe this actually means I just really care about it, and it's important to me?

This step has helped me realise that I'm better off trying and failing than sitting on my hands and not trying at all. Step 5 has made me confront the enemy – my fear of failure – and see how I need to rethink my approach, be more conscious of my mindset. Rather than let my thoughts buffet me from pillar to post unquestioned, I actually need to dictate my mindset and make it take me where I want to go, to what would bring me joy and happiness. I don't need to let fear of failing get in my way while moving toward my long-distance hiking goals.

KEY
INSIGHTS

STEP 5: CONFRONT THE ENEMY

1. Your fears are your subconscious letting you know that something is important.
2. Don't go into battle with your fears; you don't need to resolve your fears before you can move forward in your life.
3. If you give your fears more power than they deserve, they will soon convince you that they mean more than they do.
4. Don't let your fears stand in your way; you don't have to stop what you are doing or choose a different path just because you are experiencing fear.
5. Take time to understand the real source of your fears, because a life lived in fear is a life half lived.
6. Don't let the fear of disrupting your status quo stop you from making important changes in your life.
7. Become friends with your fears and allow them to come along for the ride.

JOURNAL
PROMPTS

✳ When you think of the things you want most in your life, your biggest dreams, what are the top fears that keep you from making progress on them?

✳ When you consider making changes in your life that might disrupt your status quo, what are you most afraid of? Make a note of what would genuinely be at risk and what you should stop worrying about altogether.

✳ Think about the power your fears have had in your life and the influence you have allowed them to have on your decision making. Reflect on what would be different in your life if you acknowledged these fears but didn't give them the power to influence you in any way.

STEP 6

SAY GOODBYE
TO YOUR 'BUT'

Stop being the number one
obstacle to your success, and
leave your excuses behind
once and for all.

The biggest obstacle in most people's path is themselves. They make promises they know they'll never keep and set goals that are impossible to achieve. They make excuses left, right and centre for things they haven't done and wonder why their confidence slowly drifts away.

Most people have a long list of all the reasons why their life isn't everything it could be. But the truth is, they are their own worst enemy. They set themselves up for failure by over-promising and under-delivering and by setting goals that were impossible to achieve. Or maybe they never believed they deserved to achieve those dreams in the first place.

The biggest obstacle in most people's way is themselves.

Whether they're aiming high or not so high, most people have areas of their life where they could make significant improvements – if only they would get out of their own way.

If they faced their fears and conquered their limiting beliefs. If they managed their money, took better care of their energy and were actually honest about how long things really take.

If they stopped making excuses and were actually accountable to themselves.

✱ DON'T GIVE YOURSELF AN EXCUSE TO FAIL BEFORE YOU BEGIN ✱

The first thing I want you to do is to stop undermining your self-confidence by giving yourself a get-out clause before you even begin.

Have you ever found yourself thinking about something you need or want to do only to find yourself preparing the excuse you are going to give for not getting it done – before you even get started? When you see it written down like that, it sounds like crazy behaviour, but it really is very common.

I should know, I've been guilty of it too.

When you say 'but', all you are doing
is giving yourself a get-out clause.

I'm sure if you think back even just over the last week you will be able to come up with an occasion when you said you were going to try to do something 'but ...' and had your excuse for not doing it already in place before you even began.

When you say 'but' you are giving yourself an excuse to fail before you even start.

The fact is, every time you say 'I'll try …' or 'Yeah, but …' you are preparing your personal get-out clause. It may not seem important if the things you are making excuses for are little things, but falling into the habit of excusing yourself, again and again, can have wide-reaching consequences in your life.

Every time you make an excuse for yourself you are undermining your self-belief. You may not realise it at the time, but what you are really saying to yourself is, 'I never really believed I could', 'I don't really think I can' or 'It doesn't matter if I do'.

As Yoda said: Do, or do not do – there is no try.

✳ EVERYTHING IN LIFE ✳
IS A CHOICE

From the moment you choose the clothes you put on each morning, consciously and subconsciously you are continually making choices throughout your day.

Everything in life is a choice. It doesn't always feel like it, but it's true.

When your alarm rings, you get to choose if you will hit snooze or get straight out of bed. You choose whether you should go to your meeting early or try to squeeze one more task in; whether or not you want to exercise at the end of a long, hard day; and whether you want to meet your challenges head-on or take an easier road.

Some of your options will have no right or wrong answer. Others will help your life to run smoothly and keep your day on track. But some of the choices you are presented with will mean the difference between moving forward in your life or taking one step forward and two steps back.

Own your choices instead of
excusing your excuses.

When you raise your awareness of the choices you are making throughout your day – and your life – you are able to continually take forward-moving action in your life. You will find it much easier to not say 'yes' to things you will never do, make promises you can't keep or set goals that are impossible to achieve. And if you know up front that you are likely to give up, cheat or fail to follow through you can make the conscious decision not to do it and be honest with yourself instead.

✱ FIND YOUR MISSING MOTIVATION ✱

Sometimes, knowing what changes you want and need to make in your life is not enough to make you actually do them. When that happens to you, you need to find your missing motivation.

I experienced this first hand, just last year.

After a stressful period a few years earlier I had fallen into the habit of snacking – feeding my feelings – but because the things I was snacking on were generally healthy foods, and I was distracted by the stressful events going on in my life, I hadn't been fully aware that I was doing it.

However, as you no doubt know, the unfortunate truth about diet and nutrition is that whether you are snacking on seeds and nuts, or cookies and chocolate, if you are not paying attention to the quantities you will soon pay the price around your waist.

And so, I found myself feeling much heavier than I wanted to be.

Without too much effort I was able to break my unhelpful snacking habit, but try as I might, I just couldn't shift the weight I had gained. A little came off, a little went back on again and back and forth it went. I knew I was making an effort, some of the time, but clearly I wasn't making a big enough effort enough of the time.

This seesawing of a few kilos here and a few kilos there went on for a while, and I just couldn't seem to turn the corner and get my weight back down. I wasn't making any real progress and deep down I knew I was the only one to blame.

One day while I was teaching a coaching class on values, the reason for my lack of progress hit me. I asked myself the question, 'On what level is this working for me?' and the answer wasn't at all what I expected to hear.

When it comes to health, my core values are to feel vital and energised. While I enjoy how I look and feel when I'm slim, they're not my core values, just side benefits of honouring them. Because my diet was full of healthy foods and because I was mindful of taking regular exercise and getting plenty of rest, although I was heavier than I wanted to be, I still felt vital and energised.

The reason I wasn't feeling motivated or committed to my goal was that my values were already being met.

~~~

You do not lack motivation. You just haven't aligned your intentions with your values.

I knew that if I wanted to shift the weight I had gained I was going to need to tap into different values and motives to the ones I had been concentrating on. I realised that while I felt healthy right now, if I didn't reduce my weight I could be compromising my health longer term.

My longevity.

Longevity is another one of my health values, but it wasn't one I had been thinking of when I first embarked upon my weight-loss plan. As I explored my values around vitality, energy and longevity, I realised that I had found a new source of motivation.

I realised that I wanted to feel as vital and energised at ninety as I did at fifty.

And click, like a switch, I had found a brand new source for my motivation.

✳ LET YOUR VALUES GUIDE YOU ✳

If you can't find your motivation, or you feel like you've hit a roadblock or are in a slump, you need to examine all the thoughts and feelings you have on the subject until you can identify the ones that are driving you away from your objectives instead of bringing you closer to them. Instead of allowing your hesitance to eat away at your confidence, take the time to explore what is really holding you back.

Your values are the key to
unlocking your missing motivation.

There is an expression I find very insightful – 'people do what works'. This means that whenever something is not working for you in one part of your life it is because it is serving you in some other way in another part of your life. It is this silent belief or benefit that is stopping you from moving forward in the way you would like.

An obvious example might be that you are finding it hard to get out of bed to exercise in the morning because your bed feels snuggly and warm. Ignoring your alarm 'works' because you remain cosy.

However, a subtler example might be that you are finding it hard to get out of bed because if you exercise you might lose weight, and if you lose weight, you might lose the 'excuse' you have for your life not being perfect. In this case, staying in bed 'works' because it allows you to maintain your excuses instead of facing your demons.

If you examine your beliefs and values through this lens, you will quickly be able to see what has been stopping you. Armed with your answer, you can reframe your beliefs or refine your values, and then re-engage your motivation and self-belief.

✳ MAKE SMARTER COMMITMENTS ✳

If you are finding it hard to stay on track and do what needs to get done, take some time to look at the objectives and targets you have set yourself and ask yourself if you truly believe they are achievable.

Setting unachievable goals is another major cause of demotivation, and it can make sticking to your plan of action really tough. Even if you believed your goals were achievable when you set them, with the wisdom of hindsight would you still say that they genuinely are?

～～

Nothing is more demotivating than
knowing you will never achieve
what you've said you are going to do.

If you really want to stop making excuses, commit only to goals, habits and tasks that you can't wait to achieve. Unless you create intentions that honour your values and commit to actions that are aligned with your intentions, sticking to what you said you'd do is difficult. In the next chapter we look more at how to manage your goals and expectations.

✳ SMALL STEPS CAN ✳ LEAD TO BIG RESULTS

When you are thinking about making changes or improving your life, it is easy to fall into the trap of trying to fix everything at once. You create a long list but then become so overwhelmed by it that you quickly give up. Alternatively, you may find yourself seduced by the idea of a BHAG – a big hairy audacious goal. While sometimes BHAGS can be inspiring, more often than not they are simply setting you up for failure before you even begin.

Instead of biting off more than you can chew and choking after the first or second bite, there is an easier and better way to create lasting changes in your life.

Small steps can lead to big results, so start with ten per cent.

For each of the life areas that you want to change, ask yourself, 'How could I improve this by ten per cent?' Ten per cent is the magic figure here because a ten per cent change is small enough to be easy but significant enough to notice. Once you know what a ten per cent improvement looks like in each or any of your core life areas you have the perfect starting point for creating a truly sustainable change.

Don't be afraid to take small steps –
they can still lead to big results.

This is incremental change. This is not about giving up on your boldest dreams or your biggest hopes. And it's not about being complacent about all that you could be doing with your life. The first ten per cent is just your starting point – where you will focus your attention and efforts right now.

When you've mastered your ten per cent shift and it has become natural and normal to you, if you want to further improve that aspect of your life, then and only then will it be time to ask yourself that question again. These small, ten per cent improvements will add up, and over time you will see that by taking these consistent little steps towards your ideal future, you have actually achieved a giant leap.

✳ BELIEVE IN YOURSELF ✳

If you want to shift your mindset away from one where it is okay to constantly make excuses and instead create one that supports you in meeting all your commitments with ease, as well as changing the way you think about what you do, you might also need to change the way you think about yourself.

Achievements don't just fall out of the sky, so you need to consciously choose to become the kind of person who is willing to work for what you want and who enjoys the results of their efforts.

The biggest obstacle getting between you and your motivation to do what needs to be done could actually be a lack of belief that it is worthwhile. If you can't see how your current tasks fit into your bigger picture or how they are going to take you closer to your vision for the future, it can be very hard to find the mojo to get them done.

*Your self-belief is the
secret sauce to success.*

When you find yourself feeling this way, you need to revisit your plan and see if the goals or tasks on your list are actually essential to your success. If you truly believe that they are then you need to refocus your attention on the result you will achieve, not the effort it is going to take to achieve it.

If, however, you've reviewed your list and you still can't see the point or purpose of any of the goals, it's time to delete them.

Another reason why you might find that your motivation is challenged, and you are calling on your excuses more often, is that deep down you don't really believe you can stick to what you've said you are going to do.

If you are holding on to a limiting belief about yourself and your capacity to stick at something you have set out to do, and you don't address and reframe these beliefs, it can have a big impact on your self-discipline. If there is anything in your past that you believe demonstrates you have difficulty with discipline and staying power, I want you to forget about it right now! By going over past experiences in which you have disappointed yourself or others, you will only be reaffirming the limiting belief that you lack discipline or staying power and are the kind of person who needs to keep their excuses close to hand.

Instead of anchoring your self-belief on things that have happened before – or have not happened – shift your self-talk to something more future focused. Try phrases like:

* In the past, I found it difficult to …
* Previously, I found …
* In the past, I was challenged by …

The key to each of these phrases is that you are keeping the past firmly in the past.

Sometimes the thing that is stopping you from feeling like the task at hand is worth it is that, deep down, you're not convinced that you are worth it, that you deserve to have a happy and fulfilling life.

Once you shift your mindset to one where you believe yourself to be motivated, committed, capable and deserving, you will find it a whole lot easier to leave all of your excuses behind.

MARY'S MINDSET MAKEOVER

Step 6 really hits close to home for me. I make a lot of excuses. I consider myself to be a very analytical person. I've made a career of literally finding defects and reasons not to release products. Unfortunately, since I'm hardwired to find faults, this perfectionism also applies to my own life and my goals. I can talk myself out of doing anything: exercising, dieting, working on my projects. You name it. I can even talk myself out of having fun! Since I procrastinate on the things I should be doing, I don't feel like I have any right to treat myself or have any sort of reward for the end result. Most days I feel pretty miserable about it all.

I do these kinds of things all the time. Every new year I'll join a gym and think, in order to get my money's worth, I have to go to yoga five times a week. I went once and because the class was a negative experience I never went back. So really that one class cost $795! Then I hold on to that experience and consider it an example of how I don't ever stick things out. I beat myself up that I didn't achieve that unrealistic goal. It's a cycle of excuses. But obviously my expectations were unrealistic. I was trying to start by committing to exercise straight off the bat at one hundred per cent when I should start at ten per cent. Overenthusiasm doesn't equal true motivation. And I don't have to hold on to this as a failure either; it totally doesn't define who I am.

My biggest lesson from this is: do or don't, but no buts. I used to think that saying 'I'll try' is a really good thing, but I see now that saying that without actually meaning to do it is a fantastic recipe for feeling awful. So now I'm going to commit to the things that I actually want to do that are aligned with my values and succeed in them.

No more excuses!

KEY
INSIGHTS

STEP 6: SAY GOODBYE TO YOUR 'BUT'

1. Do it, or don't do it – but don't give yourself an excuse to fail before you even begin.

2. Own your choices instead of excusing your excuses – only commit to things you can confidently achieve.

3. People do what works. If you are not making consistent progress, you need to find out the real reason why.

4. Your values can be a powerful source of motivation – let them guide you.

5. Only commit to what you really want to do; it will be easy to leave excuses behind then.

6. Small steps can lead to big leaps so start any change with a ten per cent shift.

7. Nurture your self-belief – it is the secret sauce to any success.

JOURNAL PROMPTS

✳ Think of a time you have given yourself a get-out clause or expected yourself to fail, before you even began, and what you learned from this experience.

✳ Think of a goal, habit or action you regularly find challenging to stick to or achieve. Reflect on whether it is a limit, fear or lack of commitment that is getting in your way.

✳ Think of one recurring 'but' that you are going to say goodbye to once and for all. Reflect on how your life will be different when you are no longer held back by this excuse.

STEP 7

SEE INTO THE FUTURE

Shift your focus to what you really want from life, and set clear intentions for what you do and don't want in it.

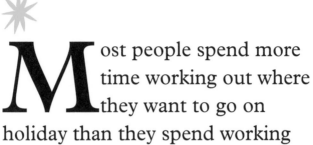

Most people spend more time working out where they want to go on holiday than they spend working out what they want from their life. But the life you want to be living won't just 'happen'. You need to define, design and plan for the life you want, to make sure it's the one you end up living.

If you want to live a happy and fulfilling life, you need to know what one looks like. In this last step we are going to shift our focus to the future and put your powerful new mindset to work as we look at what you need to focus on and what you need to let go of if you want to make your best, most brilliant life your reality.

I have always been a positive, motivated person, but there was a time when I didn't feel like I was living my best life. It all came to a head during a time that I now call my quarter-life crisis.

At the time, my life looked really good on paper. I had a well-paying corporate job and a nice boyfriend. I'd bought a house, a convertible and a *lot* of gorgeous shoes. I went on great holidays, and my life definitely looked good from the outside.

Unfortunately, on the inside, things didn't feel so great. I felt like I was living someone else's life. Someone else's good life, but someone else's life all the same.

I didn't like my job, I felt lonely when I was with my boyfriend and my shoe habit was really just another form of self-medication – a healthier one than some, but still a way of hiding from what I was feeling. I realised that the life I was living wasn't one I had consciously created. Sure, there were parts of it that I had worked very hard towards but there were other aspects that I had let 'just happen'. I also realised that if I wanted to live a more fulfilling life I was going to have to stop waiting for the things I wanted to happen and start being much more intentional about what my life contained.

I began to redesign my life.

The changes weren't instant, but over the next few years I went from earning good money in a full-time job to multiple six-figure contracts. I worked for the companies of my choice, the hours I wanted and took the holidays I needed. I left my boyfriend and met my soulmate. I moved cities, and at times it felt like I moved mountains. I lost weight, felt great and knew that I was definitely living my best life.

✳ LIVE AN INTENTIONAL LIFE ✳

I didn't just go through this process once, and it's not by accident that so far I've managed to avoid both a mummy-crisis and a mid-life one.

At the height of my corporate career, I was an in-demand troubleshooter. I was being paid incredibly well and the work was seriously challenging. But it was also all-consuming. As I started thinking about the next phase of life that I was about to enter – marriage and, hopefully, one day a family – I knew that the work I was doing wasn't compatible with what I wanted from my future life.

I went back to basics and started to think about what I wanted from my life and how it would need to change if I was to remain happy and fulfilled. I left the corporate world, completed my Professional Coaching Certification and began my life as a small business owner.

Life was really good, but ... once my son started school, I realised that running a small business had begun to feel too small for my ambitions, and so I consciously re-designed my life once again.

Living a happy and fulfilling life
doesn't happen by accident –
it happens by intention.

When I look back at the last twenty-five years, since that quarter-life crisis, I know I'm deeply happy with my life. It isn't perfect, and there are plenty of things I could improve or change, but it is happy and fulfilling because that is the intention I have set for it. But setting an intention isn't like setting a digital alarm clock – you can't set it and forget it. You need to continually and consistently make decisions that support your intention; decisions that take you closer to making your intention your reality.

❋ GIVE UP ON PERFECTION ❋

Before you get started setting those intentions, I want you to give up on any ideas you have about achieving perfection. So many people spend their lives either chasing after perfection and feeling disillusioned when they can't find it or drifting along without seeking anything and then wondering why they never discover it.

Regardless of what you see on social media, there is no such thing as a perfect life. You don't need to do it all, be it all or have it all to have a happy and fulfilling life. All you need are the things that matter most to you. Everything else is just the trimming – it's how you decorate your life.

In every rich and rewarding life, there will be successes and failures, good days and bad ones, things that you love about your life and things that you wish you didn't need to accept.

*Focus your attention on all that is
already good about your life.*

Instead of focusing on all the different ways you could improve or change your life, shift your attention to all that is good about your life. That doesn't mean you can't work to make it even better – over the last two decades I've worked on improving my life continually – but instead of making these changes or improvements your primary focus make them secondary to everything that is already good about your life instead.

✳ UNDERSTAND YOUR VALUES ✳

I've mentioned values at various points throughout this book, but I can't overstate the importance of taking the time to fully understand them. Your values are the DNA of your soul. They are the key to what matters most to you in life. Everyone has their own unique combination of values. They form part of our character and heavily influence the choices we make throughout life.

Your values are the answer to the question, 'What matters most to you in life?'

Some people think they already know the answer to this question, and they confidently list family, friends, love, money and health as their values. But to really understand your values, you need to dig a whole lot deeper than that. You need to go beyond generic values and learn to get really specific about exactly what it is about your family, friends, children, money or health that is most important to you.

By far the most common thing I hear when I teach people about values, whether it's people who are doing my Personal Happiness Prescription course or students in one of my in-depth training programs, is that they've never given their values that much thought. I even remember one woman telling me that although she knew her company values off by heart, she had no idea what her own values were.

Before you can create the life you really want,
one that is happy and fulfilling for you,
you need to know what matters most to you.

Before you can create the life you really want, one that is happy and fulfilling for you, you need to know what matters most to you – what is important in your life, and what you can happily live without. Once you know the answer to this, you can make those values front and centre in your life.

✳ GET CLEAR ABOUT WHAT ✳ YOU DON'T WANT

Once you're clear on what your values are, not only will it be easier to work out what you really want, it will be a whole lot easier to know what you don't want – and understand why you don't want it. Just like the 'old' life that I described at the beginning of this chapter, lots of things can look good. But until you have identified your values, you have no real way of knowing if they are going to feel good to you.

If knowing what you don't want is going to be positive and useful information, not just an opportunity to whinge or make kneejerk changes in your life, then it's important to be very clear on *why* you don't want it. Understanding the real reason why something is not part of your ideal future can be invaluable, saving you from chasing unfulfilling objectives and freeing up your time and energy to focus on what is really going to make you happy.

You've already detoxed your dreams in Step 1, and so you know there is no place for 'could', 'should' or 'have to' in your vision for your future. Make sure that the ideal life you are creating doesn't include things you feel you ought to be doing to keep other people happy or to fulfil some outdated ideas of what your adult life should be like.

This is your opportunity to start creating your best, most brilliant life so make sure that you leave all the unhelpful influences of your childhood, family or current work environment behind.

✳ STOP CHASING YOUR GOALS ✳

My next recommendation might sound counterintuitive, especially coming from a life coach, but I want you to stop chasing your goals.

From a young age, we are told that we need to set goals and achieve them if we want to live a happy and successful life. But the reality is that most people fail to achieve their goals most of the time – and it doesn't feel good. We blame ourselves for lacking motivation, commitment or staying power. But what if we are not the problem? What if the real problem lies with the nature of goals themselves? How we set them, when we set them, and why we set them.

I call this focus on goal achievement, and the belief that it is key to a happy and fulfilling life, the Goal Myth. I believe that buying into relentless goal setting causes you stress, erodes your self-esteem and ultimately leaves you feeling bad about yourself.

I want to be clear here. I am not anti-goals. What I am anti about is focusing on your goals as if they are the be-all and end-all. What I would like to see everyone do is put their goals back in their rightful place – as just one of the many tools available to help you get what you really want.

SMART – specific, measurable, achievable, realistic, time based – goals have their place, but the 'goalification' of ideas, ambitions and decisions that don't really need this structure only serves to undermine, demotivate or demoralise the person who is working towards them. Most of the time when you set SMART goals, they are simply a 'best guess' of what is possible. Yet people hold themselves accountable to their goals as if, having set them, their success is now guaranteed. What's worse is they believe that the reason for any resulting failure is themselves.

While achieving your goals can be motivating in the short term, failing to achieve your goals is demotivating in equal measure. Instead of focusing all your energy on your goals, you need to think about your intention: your bigger picture, your why. Once you know what your intentions are, you can then set goals, create habits and complete tasks that will bring those intentions to life.

~~~

Don't make your happiness contingent on achieving your goals.
Set intentions and commit to those instead.

I feel so strongly about this approach – this shift in focus from goals to intentions – that I developed an entire process around it called the Intention Method™ and now I train people both in how to apply it to their own life and how to teach others to change their approach too. When you follow this method, instead of leading with your goals, you begin by creating values-based intention statements about your future. Instead of picking a goal out of thin air because it seems like a good idea, you ask the question, 'What do I want to be able to say and how do I want to feel about who I am and the life I live?' When you know your answer, you can then determine the best way to fulfil your intentions – goals, habits, actions or a mix of all three.

Although goals still have a role to play, they shift in priority from being your main focus to just one of the many options available to you as you create your best, most brilliant life. If a goal you've set isn't working out for you, instead of feeling like a failure or accepting defeat, you can keep your sights firmly on your intentions and look for the next best way to fulfil them.

Focusing on your intentions in this way gives you much greater clarity, much deeper confidence and a much stronger commitment, and it will help you to keep moving forward regardless of any highs or lows you might experience along the way.

✷ BRING YOUR VISION TO LIFE ✷

Being clear about your vision, values and intentions won't just help you create your future, it will be of great benefit to the life you're living today. Instead of waiting for some perfect day in the future or for the stars to align before you can start living your ideal life, look at the essence of your ideal future and incorporate small aspects of that into your life right now.

In your vision, you might live in a home filled with fresh flowers. Bringing that future closer to your present might be as simple as spending the money you normally spend on a bottle of wine or a few drinks after work on a bunch of flowers from the supermarket.

If your ideal future includes travelling the world and experiencing different cultures, you can start by eating out in culturally diverse neighbourhoods in your home town, such as Chinatown or Little Italy, or by taking a cooking course so you can master your favourite international cuisine.

Many of the changes you can make, to bring your life closer to your vision, won't cost you very much. You might need to invest in a little extra planning and effort, but these simple actions can have an amazing impact on your sense of fulfilment in your present life. They can also help encourage and motivate you to keep working towards creating your ideal future.

I have never believed in saving up your best ideas for your 'bucket list'. I say, 'Why wait?!'

I'm not suggesting you sell your house or quit your job – although if those options are the right next step for you, then go right ahead – but waiting for decades to do the things that are important, meaningful or exciting to you is, quite frankly, ludicrous to me. Instead of saving up your biggest hopes and dreams for some far-off (or worse, never reached) point in the future, think about how you can bring that timeline forward and fulfil them sooner rather than later.

Don't save things for your bucket list.
If an experience is important to you,
make a plan to do it as soon as you possibly can.

✳ TAKE RESPONSIBILITY ✳

As you look into the future, there is one more empowering change to make, and it's all about being honest and accountable. You need to take full responsibility for creating your best, most brilliant life.

Being happy and fulfilled is the ideal way to live, but it's not something you can just wish for. If this is what you want from your life, you are going to need to commit to creating it. Realising that you are the only one responsible for your life can feel both exhilarating and terrifying. If it is up to you, there will be no-one else you can blame, but likewise, you know that no-one else can stop you either.

Take the time to understand what you don't want from life, but don't waste your time or energy focusing on it. Put your energy to better use by concentrating on the vision you have for the life you do want – and into your plan to make that vision your reality.

Stop waiting for the life you want to appear. Make the commitment each and every day to making it happen. When you hold clear intentions about what your life needs in order to be a happy and fulfilling one, it becomes easier to know what goals to set, habits to create and action to take, to make those intentions your reality.

Living your best, most brilliant life is your responsibility.
Commit to it and take your commitment seriously.

DAVID'S MINDSET MAKEOVER

One of the key takeaways for me is there's no such thing as a perfect life, so I should aim for a brilliant one instead. I'm going to spend a lot of time on Step 7. I'm going to really set my intentions, then circle back to Step 1 and go through it all over again, to make sure I can identify what things I can modify in my life to really make sure I'm living my best life. Then I can move forward with my newly designed, defined and planned best life because it won't just happen – I do have to work on it, which is something I haven't done in the past. There's no point just dreaming or focusing on what is a 'perfect' life – because it doesn't exist.

I've often been plagued by chasing perfection, and many times I have felt disillusioned by not getting it or finding it. And I've now realised that many of these goals have been driven by financial numbers. And the fact that I haven't achieved them left me feeling empty and, at times, like a failure.

But I have to think about my true values. Are goals driven by financial ambitions really what matter to me? Being a perfectionist by nature, I've wanted everything to work out exactly as I wanted and planned. And even though I've had good things – opening my own fitness club and making it successful – there's still something missing.

I now realise my values are not tied to things that are purely financially driven. Step 7 has allowed me to refocus on what I really want. I've identified five clear intentions and realised my main values are about family, friends and loved ones – about allocating more quality time with them, doing simple things. Because ultimately that's what makes me more happy in my real life. Chasing an illusion will get me nowhere. I've got to live with intention.

KEY
INSIGHTS

STEP 7: SEE INTO THE FUTURE

1. Living your best, most brilliant life won't happen by accident. It happens when you set clear intentions.
2. There is no such thing as a perfect life, so give up on perfection and focus on living a happy and fulfilling life.
3. Take time to understand your values – the things that matter most to you.
4. Get clear about what you don't want – so you don't waste any time chasing it.
5. Don't fall for the goal myth. It's time to stop thinking that your goals are the be-all and end-all and start focusing on your intentions instead.
6. Instead of waiting for some perfect day in the future, bring your vision to life with small, easy changes you can make right away.
7. The only person responsible for your life is you, and you've got this!

JOURNAL
PROMPTS

❋ What are three things you want more of in your life that you hadn't fully considered or realised until now?

❋ What are the top five things that matter most to you in life? On a scale of 1 to 10 how well represented are these values in your life right now?

❋ Map out the perfect day, where you are living a life aligned with your values and intentions and doing what you truly want.

A FINAL WORD
FROM DOMONIQUE

Congratulations on working your way through these 7 Steps. We've covered a lot of ground, and I'm proud of you for all the mindset shifts you've had so far and excited about the resulting changes you are going to see in your life.

It will always be easier to have an ordinary life, and as I said right back when we started, most people are 'fine' with fine, and 'okay' with okay.

I'm so glad you're not.

I'm glad you decided to show up and learn how to create the mindset you need to make living your happiest and most fulfilling life your reality.

You deserve to live your best, most brilliant life – not just some day but every day – and by applying the lessons you've learned in this book, I'm confident you're well on your way!

PS: I'd love to know what your biggest insights and your favourite mindset shifts have been throughout the *7 Step Mindset Makeover*. You can find me on Instagram or Facebook at domoniquebertolucci; pop on over and say hello and tell me about the mindset shifts you've been experiencing.

PPS: If you never got around to downloading the workbook created to go with this book, you can still access it free at domoniquebertolucci.com/mindset-makeover. I've included summaries of each chapter, exercises and expanded journal prompts to help you go deeper, plus a few extra goodies.

ACKNOWLEDGEMENTS

My first thanks, as always, go to my wonderful agent, Tara Wynne at Curtis Brown. When we met all those years ago, sharing my ideas with people from all around the world was just a dream. I am grateful every single day for your belief in me.

Thanks to Pam Brewster for sharing my vision with this new series, to Brooke Munday and all the team at Hardie Grant for giving my books such a wonderful home, to Regine Abos for creating the gorgeous design that brings this new Mindset Matters series to life, and to my editor Kate Daniel for polishing my words with such love and care. Thank you to Karen Yates and Stephanie Van Schilt for helping me to bring the original concept to life.

To my readers who connect with me in my Facebook group and on Instagram, thank you for sharing your experiences or simply stopping by to say hello. I am so inspired by the way you put my words into action in your life, and hearing from you always makes my day.

To the wonderful Holly Kahmal who has given me the most priceless thing of all – more time. Your support has been invaluable and enabled me to achieve so much more than I ever could on my own. To Annette, Anomie, Gioula, Helen, Kerri and Jennifer thank you for putting your trust in me and becoming the first Intention Method™ Certified Coaches.

To Renata, Jo, Jodi and Milly, thank you for welcoming me back with open arms, and to Brooke – it always feels like I never left. To Carrie, my fellow peanut, thank you for all the wit and giggles and for generally keeping me sane.

To my dearest Dame Soul Sisters AM, thank you for the million and one WhatsApp laughs and the two hundred plus years of combined friendship we share.

To Lisa and Tony, Polly and Charles, Claire and Chris, Esther and Mark thank you for being my family. I miss you. Celebrations aren't the same without you (and a bottle of Veuve or two).

To Mum, Dad and Jeff and Julie, thank you for your unconditional love and support. You will never know how much it means to me. To Lara, Josh, Isabelle and Benjy for all your love and hugs.

To my darling Sophia and precious Toby, writing a book during the school holidays might never have been easy, but writing during school holidays in a lockdown was a whole new challenge. That you have both been so supportive and respectful of my work has warmed my heart. I feel like I must be the luckiest person in the world because I get to be your mum.

And to Paul, there are so many different ways that you show your love and support for me, so once again I want to say thank you for everything, always.

ABOUT THE AUTHOR

Domonique Bertolucci is the bestselling author of *The Happiness Code: Ten keys to being the best you can be* and seven other books about happiness: what it is, how to get it and, most importantly, how to keep it.

Domonique has spent the last twenty-five years working with large companies, dynamic small businesses and everyday people, teaching them how to get more happiness, more success and more time just to catch their breath.

Prior to starting her own business in 2003, Domonique worked as a model and then in the cut-throat world of high finance, where she gained a reputation as a strategic problem solver and dynamic leader. In her final corporate role, she was the most senior woman in a billion-dollar company.

Domonique's readership spans the English-speaking world, and her workshops, online courses and coach training programs are attended by people from all walks of life from all around the globe – people who want more out of life at home, at work and everywhere in between.

As well as being an accomplished professional speaker, Domonique is the host of three top-rated Audible Original Podcasts. She has given hundreds of interviews across all forms of media including television, radio, print and digital media; more than 10 million people have seen, read or heard her advice.

When she is not working, Domonique's favourite ways of spending her time are with her husband and two children, reading a good book and keeping up the great Italian tradition of feeding the people that you love.

Domonique jokes that she has nearly as many passports as James Bond. She is Australian by birth, Italian by blood and British by choice. She is currently based in Sydney, Australia.

OTHER BOOKS BY DOMONIQUE

The Happiness Code: Ten keys to being the best you can be
Love Your Life: 100 ways to start living the life you deserve
100 Days Happier: Daily inspiration for life-long happiness
Less is More: 101 ways to simplify your life
The Kindness Pact: 8 promises to make you feel good about who you are and the life you live
The Daily Promise: 100 ways to feel happy about your life
You've Got This: 101 ways to boost your confidence, nurture your spirit and remind yourself that everything is going to be okay
9 Step Negativity Detox: Reset your mindset and love your life

GUIDED JOURNALS BY DOMONIQUE

Live more each day: A journal to discover what really matters
Be happy each day: A journal for life-long happiness

FREE RESOURCES

You can download a range of free tools, templates and extra resources designed to help you to live your best, most brilliant life at domoniquebertolucci.com/life

KEEP IN TOUCH WITH DOMONIQUE

domoniquebertolucci.com

facebook.com/domoniquebertolucci

instagram.com/domoniquebertolucci

Join Domonique's private Facebook group for regular discussion, insights and inspiration to help you get more out of life.

Facebook.com/groups/domoniquebertolucci

FOR MORE INFORMATION

Find out more about Domonique's life coaching courses and programs: domoniquebertolucci.com/programs

Find out more about Domonique's training, certification and corporate programs: domoniquebertolucci.com/training